W9-BND-459

The
CONNECTED
Educator

Learning and Leading in a Digital Age

SHERYL NUSSBAUM-BEACH
LANI RITTER HALL

Solution Tree | Press

a division of

Solution Tree

Copyright © 2012 by Solution Tree Press

All rights reserved, including the right of reproduction of this book in whole or in part in any form.

555 North Morton Street
Bloomington, IN 47404

800.733.6786 (toll free) / 812.336.7700
FAX: 812.336.7790

email: info@solution-tree.com
solution-tree.com

Visit **go.solution-tree.com/technology** to download materials related to this book.

Printed in the United States of America

15 14 13 12   2 3 4 5

Library of Congress Cataloging-in-Publication Data

Nussbaum-Beach, Sheryl.
  The connected educator : learning and leading in a digital age / Sheryl Nussbaum-Beach, Lani Ritter Hall.
     p. cm.
  Includes bibliographical references and index.
  ISBN 978-1-935543-17-6 (perfect bound) -- ISBN 978-1-935543-18-3 (library edition)
  1. Teachers--In-service training. 2. Professional learning communities. 3. Digital communications. I. Title.
  LB1731.N87 2012
  370.71'1--dc23
                    2011036345

Solution Tree
Jeffrey C. Jones, CEO & President

Solution Tree Press
President: Douglas M. Rife
Publisher: Robert D. Clouse
Vice President of Production: Gretchen Knapp
Managing Production Editor: Caroline Wise
Copy Editor: Sarah Payne-Mills
Proofreader: Rachel Rosolina
Text Designer: Amy Shock
Cover Designer: Jenn Taylor

ACC LIBRARY SERVICES AUSTIN, TX

For Gus:

You have believed in, supported, encouraged, and pushed me to be my best me. With your being there, your honesty, your understanding all the hours spent on the computer, your listening and giving feedback—I am here. I will always be grateful.

—Lani

For Amber, Heidi, Noah, and Grace:

Because of you I have become who I am today. Because of you I was driven to want an education, to be a better person, and to fall deeply and passionately in love with learning. Thank you for being such good teachers and wonderful children.

—Sheryl (a.k.a. Mom)

Acknowledgments

Our first acknowledgment is to the power of a connected collegial relationship and the technology that made that relationship and this book possible. Two connected learner leaders, separated geographically by more than five hundred miles, availed themselves of technology to collaborate, share insights, and generate ideas. Using Skype led to words flowing on Google Docs as each chapter of this book emerged and evolved. The priceless comment feature enabled the unpacking and repacking that brought us to this place. Interestingly, in the spirit of connected learning, neither this book nor its ideas touched paper until now in its final form. The drafts, edits, collaboration, brainstorming all were done online in the cloud.

Amber Karnes, Sheryl's daughter, kept us organized, provided support and expertise that enabled us to create meaningful graphics, offered thoughtful feedback, and read and reread all our edits as she pushed us to clearer description and illuminated understanding. Amber, you allowed us to focus clearly on our mission of helping readers understand the potential connected learning communities have to transform education. We are also deeply grateful for the time, energy, coffee, and ideas you added to the process. Your willingness to intercept phone calls, push Sheryl to cut off Skype, close TweetDeck, quit checking Facebook, and to focus, focus, focus on writing enabled this book to become a reality. Thank you for making the final formatting changes and helping us ship. Amber, we are forever in your debt.

We have benefited from the ideas of a multitude of connected learners in our networks and communities. You will read conversations from Sheryl's Twitter network, perspectives and insights gleaned from our personal learning networks, and examples of collaboration and trust building from the online communities of practice we lead and learn in at Powerful Learning Practice (PLP). To our personal learning networks and our PLPeeps, thank you for your transparency, for your passion, for your sharing. We have learned so much from you, and you have been invaluable to this collaboration.

It would be impossible for us to acknowledge all those who have influenced the trajectory of our lives and our thinking as we came to this place. Yet there are those without whom we would not be here today. Lani would like to thank her father and mother for instilling a love of learning; Paul Karlin for providing an opportunity to become a teacher leader; and Anne Davis for sharing her wisdom and collaborations and for encouraging Lani to expand her connections. Sheryl would like to thank her family (Amber and Jimmy; Heidi, Mark, and Luke; Noah and Sarah; Grace and Chris; Travis, David, Itchy, and Bane) for being there for her when she needed them most; Will Richardson, for long conversations about educational truth, for laughter and more laughter, and for pushing her thinking in so many ways; John Norton for being her mentor and life coach and for helping with the book through the numerous reads, rereads, and editing suggestions; and all the Powerful Learning Practice staff for the selfless acts they commit on behalf of others every day.

To our students of the past and the students of the future, thank you for all you have taught us and for being the light that has guided our way. Thoughts of you compel us to resist urges to finish prematurely and to instead engage in deep reflection as we encourage others to become connected learners and leaders.

Lastly, we want to express appreciation for each other. When we began, many expressed concern that we were collaborating on this project; they warned of stress, of differing opinions, of hard conversations that could not be resolved. This process has further cemented both a deep collegial relationship and a true friendship. We are grateful for all we bring to each other.

—Lani and Sheryl

Solution Tree Press would like to thank the following reviewers:

Alec Couros
Associate Professor, Information and
  Communication Technologies
Faculty of Education, University of
  Regina
Regina, Saskatchewan

Anne Davis
Retired Educator
J. H. House Elementary and Georgia
  State University
Atlanta, Georgia

William M. Ferriter
Sixth-Grade Teacher
Salem Middle School
Apex, North Carolina

William Kist
Associate Professor, Curriculum and
  Instruction
Kent State University
Kent, Ohio

John Norton
Education Writer and Editor
Little Switzerland, North Carolina

Meg Ormiston
Author and Consultant
Tech Teachers, Inc.
Burr Ridge, Illinois

Kathy Schrock
Educational Technology Coach
Kathy Schrock's Guide for Educators
Eastham, Massachusetts

Jennifer Schuelke
Seventh-Grade Language Arts Teacher
Canyon Ridge Middle School
Austin, Texas

Cortney Steffens
First-Grade Teacher
Cherry Lane Elementary School
Suffern, New York

Visit **go.solution-tree.com/technology** to
download materials related to this book.

Table of Contents

About the Authors

Sheryl Nussbaum-Beach is a veteran twenty-year educator. She has been a classroom teacher, technology coach, charter school principal, district administrator, university instructor, and digital learning consultant. Currently, she is completing her dissertation for her doctorate in educational planning, policy, and leadership at the College of William and Mary.

She is the owner and founder of 21st Century Collaborative, LLC, a digital learning consulting business through which she regularly delivers keynotes and workshops, along with supporting nonprofits in their grant work. Through Powerful Learning Practice, which she cofounded with Will Richardson, she works with schools and districts from across the United States, Canada, New Zealand, Norway, and Australia to re-envision their learning cultures and communities.

Sheryl is a sought-after presenter at national and international events, speaking on topics of 21st century reform, teacher and educational leadership, community building, and educational issues impacting marginalized populations such as the homeless.

Sheryl lives near the Atlantic Ocean and spends her spare time playing on the water with her four children and dachshunds Itchy, Bane, and Abby. To learn more about Sheryl's work, visit her website at http://21stcenturycollaborative.com, check out http://plpnetwork.com, or follow her on Twitter @snbeach.

Lani Ritter Hall has more than thirty-five years of diverse teaching experiences in urban, suburban, and independent schools at the middle and secondary level in the United States and Canada. She and her students began collaborating globally in the 1980s using a curriculum she designed and developed. Lani, a National Board Certified Teacher, has created and facilitated professional development around technology infusion into learning for more than twenty years and has presented at local, state, and national conferences. She has expanded her global collaborations through her leadership role in the initial years of K12Online, the first educator-led, free, totally online conference; her participation in the first massive open online course that explored connectivism and connective knowledge; and through her current roles of community leader and codirector of connected coaches in online communities of practice for Powerful Learning Practice.

Lani earned a bachelor's degree in political science from Earlham College and a master's degree in curriculum and instruction from Cleveland State University. She lives with her husband in Northeast Ohio. To learn more about Lani's work, visit her blog Possibilities Abound (http://possibilitiesabound.blogspot.com), or follow her on Twitter @lanihall.

To book Sheryl or Lani for professional development, contact pd@solution-tree .com.

Introduction

Things do not change; we change.
—Henry David Thoreau

"Every time I go to school, I have to power down," a high school student told researchers. This riveting statement, quoted by 21st century learning advocate Marc Prensky (2001, p. 7), has been cited thousands of times in magazine articles, books, blogs, speeches, and slideshows. Most of us would agree that kids *do* have to power down when they come to school. The most disturbing aspect of this quote, however, is that Prensky cited this cautionary message *more than a decade ago*. Yet it remains relevant in far too many schools right now. Do high school students feel any differently today than that student did at the turn of the millennium? In some trailblazing schools, yes, they do. But many observers, inside and outside education, still ask, as edublogger Ryan Bretag did in 2007, "Will we ever reach a point where students say, 'When I go to school, I have to power *up*'?"

The Disconnect

With the advent of social media, learning occurs anytime, anywhere, and students regularly pursue knowledge in networked and collaborative ways—with or without us. Emerging web technologies connect young people in ways never before possible. They learn from each other outside the classroom through smartphones, text messaging, and social networking sites such as blogs, Twitter, YouTube, Facebook, Google+, and Flickr—the list grows longer every day. The big question is, What impact does the growth of social media have on learning inside the classroom?

Think about it. Students are growing up in an environment where they control the flow of information, how they receive it, and the format in which it comes to them—all with the click of a few buttons. Today's children have grown up with remote control everything, constant communication, and instant access to information in entertaining formats. It's as if they are wired into existence through their mobile technologies, no longer tethered, but instead operating as free-range learners. They passionately consume media and are riveted to the things that interest them online. Their world encourages connectedness. They expect a continuous connection with their family and friends and the world at large.

Everywhere they go, students are moving toward the future at full speed. For example, Sheryl's daughter has a new car that talks to her, adjusts the interior lighting when the brightness outside changes, and even parks itself. The global GPS network makes sure no one gets lost. She can simply tap into it using one of many devices, including smartphones. Then our kids get to school and find themselves locked in the past. Bells signal the beginning and end of class, cell phones must be off, desks are in straight rows, teachers lecture on and on, and paper textbooks are filled with preselected information presented in a convergent, linear format. No wonder students feel a disconnect.

Each year through its "Speak Up" surveys, Project Tomorrow documents the increasingly significant disparity between students' aspirations for using technology for learning and the attitudes of their less technology-comfortable teachers and administrators (Project Tomorrow, 2010). Students, regardless of community demographics, socioeconomic backgrounds, gender, or grade, tell researchers that the lack of sophisticated use of emerging technology tools in school is holding back their education and, in many instances, disengaging them from learning.

Although the technological revolution has permeated every other area of society, education—often viewed as a reflection of our culture and values—has been left largely untouched. Schools have mostly resisted the potential of wireless connectivity to shift away from teacher-centered pedagogy. The networked landscape of learning that is readily available to many students and adults *outside* of school challenges us to re-envision what we do *inside* our schools and classrooms—or risk a growing irrelevance in students' lives.

This book addresses where educators fit into the picture. What shifts do we need in education to make sense of learning in a world of constant change? What should professional development look like in the 21st century? What beyond traditional "sit and get" experiences can help us help children become conscientious global learners and leaders? When will every educator be able to say, "When I pursue professional learning, I have to power *up*"?

Professional Development for the 21st Century

Although many national organizations call for schools to teach 21st century skills and for a shift to learning communities rather than traditional classrooms, few models exist to help educators become co-learners with their students.

As part of our own growth as teacher learners, we have used the web to develop and connect to a personal learning network—a group of knowledgeable colleagues and recognized experts who are also eager to learn and to share what they know.

As we thought about changes for teacher learning, in March 2010, Sheryl used the microblog Twitter to pose this query to her personal learning network: "How would you describe professional development in the 21st century?" Within minutes, a variety of interesting responses poured in—all using 140 characters or less.

- "I can tell you it needs to be available any time, anywhere, on a variety of platforms . . ." *Steve Anderson, @web20classroom*

- "PD in the 21st Century? Highly personalized." *Beth Still, @bethstill*

- "Necessary, invigorating, available, active, connected, complicated." *Mel Hutch, @melhutch*

- "No more sitting in rows and chairs. It no longer comes to you, you MUST search it out and be involved in FINDING best practice." *Carol Broos, @musictechie*

- "I'd describe PD in the 21st Century as an integral and defining part of almost any job. It's also part of being literate today." *David Warlick, @dwarlick*

- "PD in 21st Century—learning from a PLN, putting that learning to use and documenting it—sharing with others as you grow." *Leslie Maniotes, @lesliemaniotes*

- "PD in 21st C: targeted, personalized but communal, active, action research, transparent . . ." *Derrick Willard, @derrickwillard*

- "As personal pd—a shift away from state/district/school pd with the onus on accessing multiple inputs using variety of platforms." *Cory Plough, @mrplough07*

- "For me PD is customized, immersive, ubiquitous, self-constructed, community based, empowering, & connective (I know . . . many adjectives.)" *Wendy Drexler, @wendydrexler*

- "It's available 24/7 if one wants it. Its reach is regional, national, and global." *Hiram Cuevas, @cuevash*

- "21 Cen teacher PD is blended, ongoing, relevant, job-embedded, collaborative and a combination of self-directed + informed by data." *Tania Sterling, @taniasterling*

- "Unattached. No rooms, few boundaries. Blend of the old ways (for those that can't let go) and the new ways (for those that need to jump ahead)." *Tim Holt, @timholt2007*

The Need for Change

Professional development needs to change. We know this.

A revolution in technology has transformed the way we can find each other, interact, and collaborate to create knowledge as connected learners. What are connected learners? Learners who collaborate *online*; learners who use social media to connect with others around the globe; learners who engage in conversations in safe online spaces; learners who bring what they learn online back to their classrooms, schools, and districts.

The digital era puts us in a position to collectively reimagine learning and to transform education into an experience with lasting relevance to the 21st century student. The potential to form global networks of digital learners has barely been tapped. Virtual learning communities have the potential to transform professional learning to produce progress and innovation on behalf of our students and ourselves.

Technology and the virtual universe are transforming the way we do most tasks in our daily lives. The time has come to reject incremental change and to radically *transform* education to reflect the current global community. Teachers must learn to model connectedness and enable students to develop personal learning networks, made up of people and resources from both their physical and virtual worlds—but first teachers must become connected collaborators themselves. The need for teachers to fully exploit the transformative potential of emerging learning technologies—and to do it within a global framework—is the focus of *The Connected Educator*.

Join Us

To all learners—educators, teachers, administrators, curriculum developers, parents, and students—who have not yet considered the benefits of network and community participation, who have just dipped a toe into the torrent of opportunity, or who are already immersed in digital tools, we ask you to explore with us the power of connected, self-directed professional learning.

Help us remix the concepts of professional learning communities, personal learning networks, and communities of practice to support lifelong learning. Make use of and extend our suggested applications. Commit with us to develop a shared wisdom that supports *teachers and leaders as learners first*. As we offer our expertise to each other and work to solve problems collaboratively, we will build collective intelligence. This new way of learning will set our children on the road to a life of passion-driven, connected learning.

What Is Different About This Book?

This book is a journey into what it means to be *a learner first* and an educator second. It is a book about you, about your professional learning. It's also about us— the collective *us* in education—and how our own learning can transform student learning through a systemic vision of professional development.

We draw on the research base and the demonstrated success (including our own) of learning in networks, communities, and teams to propose a powerful, collaborative concept we call *connected learning communities,* an idea we will develop more fully in chapter 2 and throughout the book. The book draws heavily on our experience as members and leaders of connected learning communities for nearly a decade—and from work with numerous learning communities through Powerful Learning Practice, a professional development company cofounded by Sheryl and educator and author Will Richardson. At the time of this printing, Powerful Learning Practice has served more than four thousand educators in schools around the world.

In this book, we integrate what is currently working in schools with a new model of professional development. This model shifts the locus of control to you, the connected learner, rather than vesting it in outsiders, higher-ups, and professional development consultants who may have good content but lack your school context. Our intent is to help you, as well as the partners, parents, and policymakers who support you, improve learning and teaching in and beyond the classroom walls.

How to Get the Most Out of This Book

This book is an interactive professional development journey that not only shares best practices, dynamic examples of network and community creation, and the development of meaningful connections but also seeks reciprocity in sharing from you, the reader.

If connected learning is new to you, this may be the type of book you want to first scan through, and then go back and read chapter by chapter while you ponder, take notes, and think deeply. It's OK to travel slowly, if need be. However, passively reading this book will not give you the same learning opportunity as active involvement. We encourage you to jump in and try the suggested activities as a way to begin building your own connectedness as a 21st century learner. Also, visit **go.solution-tree.com/technology** for live links to the URLs mentioned in text and other materials associated with the book. You do not have to take on all the tasks at once—just start somewhere!

Each chapter is divided into three sections that explain the concepts associated with connected learning and give hands-on practice suggestions.

1. Each chapter begins with Our Stories in which we share a personal example based on our experiences in leading and learning in networks and communities.

2. A content section follows that unpacks the ideas being developed. We offer a few takeaway points or questions to consider in the Where Are We? and Where to Now? sections.

3. Finally, we ask you to Get Connected by participating in an authentic application that completes each chapter. This is a *crowdsourcing activity,*

that is, an activity in which readers come together in a virtual space and add to the collective knowledge of what is being discussed. You will learn to be a connected learner not only by reading about connected learning but by doing what connected learners do—co-constructing meaning and knowledge.

Throughout the book, be on the lookout for Think About sections, where we ask you to reflect on the ideas in the book, and Putting It in Practice sections, which have practical applications of the concepts in this book. The Get Connected sections help you collectively use tools through immersion. But our primary focus is the human aspect—people connecting through communities of learners, which these tools support.

- **Chapter 1:** The goal of this chapter is to *set the stage for understanding what it is to be a connected learner.* We address the importance of collaboration for the connected learner and how collaboration differs from cooperation. We've included a self-evaluation rubric so you can determine where you stand as a literate 21st century learner. Finally, we'll show you what a typical day in the life of a connected learner looks like.

- **Chapter 2:** We *make a case for connected learning in communities.* We look at a new approach to professional development. We explain why professional learning communities or online networks alone are not powerful enough to create the kind of shift needed in education today. In appendix A (page 153), we include the research foundation and the experience base from which our ideas for connected learning have emerged; in this chapter, we give a glimpse of their evolution.

- **Chapter 3:** We *explore the importance of seeing yourself as a learner first, educator second.* We consider how educators leverage connected learning communities to serve the interests of 21st century learners.

- **Chapter 4:** We *look at developing a collaborative culture and a mindset that supports connected learning.* We talk about the importance of online, collaborative relationships and how to develop and maintain trust in a virtual relationship. We describe collegial relationships in which connected educators share ideas and challenge each other's thinking, working toward a common vision.

- **Chapter 5:** We *invite you to explore free and affordable technologies and virtual environments* that support collaborative learning. We introduce you to Web 2.0 tools—video-sharing sites, social bookmarking tools, blogs, wikis, and podcasts—as conduits to deep learning. We cover tools for documenting and archiving, connecting and collaborating, and extending learning outside the classroom.

- **Chapter 6:** We *guide you through the steps of implementing a connected learning community.* This includes the characteristics of a healthy community, conditions that encourage the emergence of a connected learning community, and how to take the first step in designing your own personal learning network. We discuss what to watch for as your connected learning community matures.

- **Chapter 7:** We *examine how to sustain the momentum of professional learning* by using *scale* as a strategy for co-creating and improving a learning community. We also address how to evaluate learning that takes place in connected spaces.

- **Chapter 8:** We *focus on leadership—system, school, and teacher leadership—in a distributed model.* We redefine the teacher as leader and point to the need to empower students as leaders. Finally, we address moving from mandated to mutual accountability with student leaders.

- **Chapter 9:** We *look at what the future holds* for the connected learner and what being a connected learner means for *you.*

Terms, Definitions, and Resources

To help with unfamiliar terminology in this book, we have included a glossary (page 147) for your convenience, and as stated, in appendix A, we have included the research basis for the concepts we explore. In appendix B (page 163), we've provided a practical, real-world example of how scale (discussed in chapter 7) affects a project. We have also collected definitions and resources in an online, social bookmarking tool called Diigo. We ask you to bookmark resources using common tags so that, together, we can create a dynamic resource list for each chapter. A list of common Twitter and Diigo tags is included in appendix C (page 167).

Contributing to the Get Connected activities at the end of each chapter will help this book become a collaborative journey into professional learning. With your help, *The Connected Educator* will continue to expand and remain relevant in the future as we co-construct and make sense of all we learn.

Jump in and get connected with us. Who knows what spontaneous collaborations will result from your participation.

Chapter One

Defining the Connected Educator

Our lives are connected by a thousand invisible threads.

—Herman Melville

Our Stories

Back in the early 1990s, I was teaching children's literature to preservice educators at Valdosta State College (now Valdosta State University). I wanted to help students extend their reach beyond our small-town, south-Georgia culture and experience firsthand the power of connecting and collaborating with people and cultures very different from their own. I believed that if they were changed because of such connections, they would pass similar experiences on to their future students. I put the word out on the online bulletin boards where I regularly engaged in threaded discussions and asked all individuals interested in sharing their culture with preservice teachers in a virtual global exchange to email me. I was astounded by the number of responses. Using a geographical list created from the responses I received over just a few days, I had students choose an area and then matched each to an international partner for correspondence through Internet Relay Chat, bulletin boards, and email—the cutting-edge collaboration tools of the day. They were to gather information to create a model classroom learning station, sharing stories, artifacts, and children's literature from their partner's country.

The results were more incredible than anything I ever could have imagined. Because these teachers had built relationships and learned in a social context, they gave the assignment outstanding effort. Many of the global online partners sent children's books or other items representing their country's culture for the preservice teachers to share. The outcomes were so impressive that the local chapter of the International Reading Association asked the class to stage a Children's Literature Day in a store space at the local mall. The teachers dressed in costumes native to the country they represented and created activities around the children's books from those countries. It was a day of learning for the entire city.

Since then, my belief in networking as a means of deep, sustained learning has not only grown but has been validated by experience. The tools have changed, but the principle has remained the same: we need one another. Theories of social learning—the learning that occurs within a social context such as school-based learning communities, online networks, or serendipitous connection—suggest that people learn best from one another.

—Sheryl

We love the way Cisco (2007) describes the world we live in today. It puts the focus of networks where it should be—on the human aspect:

> Welcome, welcome to a brand-new day. A new way of getting things done. . . . Where people subscribe to people, not magazines. And the team you follow, now follows you. Welcome to a place where books rewrite themselves. Where you can drag and drop people wherever they want to go. And a phone doubles as a train ticket, plane ticket, or a lift ticket. . . . Where a home video is experienced everywhere at once. Where a library travels across the world. . . . And we're more powerful together than we could ever be apart. . . . Welcome to the human network.

Technology makes connecting and collaborating so easy. But *most* important are the relationships that learning technologies make possible.

People connect through communities of learners, which today's technological tools support in new ways. Through technology, learning is seamless. Learning can take place anywhere, any time. However, the technologies, while exciting and motivating, are secondary to you—the connected learner.

Yet in most schools, still, the assumptions are that learning is an individual process, that learning has a beginning and an end, that learning happens in schools separately from the rest of life's activities, and that learning is the result of teaching. Technology is beginning to shift those assumptions and change the way we, as educators, learn.

If you have not yet begun to thin the walls and open the doors of your classroom, school, or district, you're most likely plagued with the same nagging feeling we started with: *something is missing.* Educators have accepted and perpetuated professional practice behind shut doors and in closed buildings, our day-to-day work disconnected from colleagues' efforts. We have read, we have listened, and we have been talked at. We have done the best we could do given the resources available. So *what* are we missing? *Meaningful collaboration and authentic collegiality.* But, before describing this missing piece in our professional lives, we must first explore an important way to approach it.

Do-It-Yourself Learning

As a connected educator, you have the opportunity to direct your learning, connect, collaborate, and grow your professional practice. Connected learners adopt a do-it-yourself (DIY) mentality. *Do-it-yourself* is a term traditionally used to describe building, modifying, or repairing something without aid from experts or professionals. In the 21st century, it means so much more.

The do-it-yourself movement signals a shift away from dependency and obsessive consumerism toward a *learner first* attitude, one of self-reliance and a can-do spirit. Examples of grassroots political and social activism abound: in bold business start-ups, self-publishing, and independent music, art, and film. Individuals are pushing themselves to learn for themselves rather than be taught by someone else. This paradigm is spilling over into the way educators learn.

The idea of orchestrating your own learning, selecting your own mentors, organizing your own conferences and workshops, and pursuing just-in-time learning has taken off around the globe. All this is possible because we live in what some are calling a participatory culture (Jenkins, 2006), or remix culture, when we build on the work others have shared in order to make it better.

It is relatively easy today to become a producer of information rather than just a consumer. In the era of connectivity, informal mentoring relationships are easily formed and those with expertise are eager to pass on what they know to novices. In a participatory culture, I am unable to learn from you if you are not sharing online. I will never be able to find you and leverage what you know.

Becoming a connected, do-it-yourself learner begins with your willingness to be a findable, clickable, searchable-on-Google person who shares openly and transparently. From there we can form a connection, a conversation, a relationship and begin to collaborate.

The New Collaboration

Collaborative problem solving is as old as fireside chats in the cave. Our families frequently sit around the breakfast or dinner table solving problems together. Wide-net collaborative problem solving in real time is simply an extension of such collaboration. As connected learners, we do not have to personally know the people in our network to coconstruct and collaborate with them, thanks to today's powerful and ubiquitous technologies. Because of that, connected learning carries a huge payoff for the learner. We can reach out to our network, harvest the collective wisdom found there, and then bring it back to the school.

As noted previously, we are so often missing meaningful collaboration and authentic collegiality in our professional lives. Only rarely and briefly have we experienced the rush of satisfaction that results from purposeful conversations around teaching and learning that produce positive changes in our practice. Meaningful collaboration and collegiality are forces that can bring about the kind of shift we all are seeking in schools today—a shift that connects and engages us as educators, supports and sustains us, and helps us enrich our students' lives and accelerate their achievement.

How do we define *collaboration*? We have found that educators often confuse collaboration with *cooperation*. Cooperative learning is an instructional strategy in which everyone in the learning group performs a unique role to accomplish a common task. Each learner works individually on the same topic and then shares with the group what he or she learned in order to deepen everyone's understanding. Because the work is done individually (although often graded as a group), one learner's failure to participate does not negatively affect the outcome or learning for the entire group.

Cooperation is an individual approach to knowledge construction done within a group. We all contribute something that any of us could have contributed if asked. As educators, we are used to working with one another, used to cooperating to produce some degree of combined effort on students' behalf. It's the collaboration piece that seems to be missing in most schools.

Collaboration occurs when we approach goals as connected learners, relying on each other's skills, knowledge, talents, and readiness to share. When individual contributions make a significant difference in the final outcome of the work or learning, when we each share from our own specific knowledge and gifts, collaboration occurs. In other words, each of us brings something unique to the project or task that couldn't have happened without our involvement. The simple truth is that *there is a limit to how much we can learn if we keep to ourselves* (Fullan & Hargreaves, 1991). By deepening our connectedness to the level of true collaboration, we can best meet the needs of today's students. Figure 1.1 illustrates cooperation versus collaboration.

Personal knowledge building is important in a collaborative culture, in part because it adds to the value we bring to the collective space. In fact, without regularly investing in our individual learning, collaboration is just posturing and one more way to maintain the status quo. We first have to invest in personal knowledge building before we will have knowledge to share.

Technology makes connecting, collaborating, and learning easier than ever before in human history. In fact, 21st century technologies make possible relationships that once were unimaginable. They create a new potential for collaboration that can lead to powerful collective problem solving.

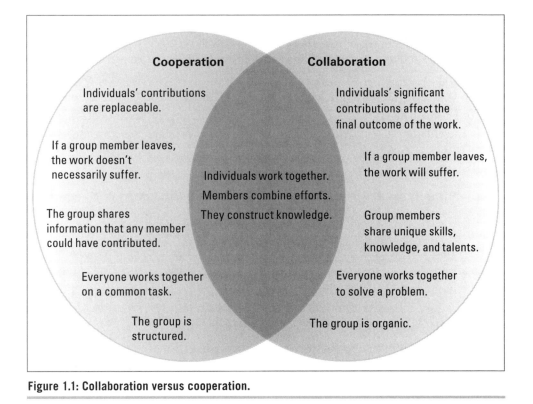

Figure 1.1: Collaboration versus cooperation.

Think About

Have you moved beyond cooperation? What role is collaboration playing in your professional learning and your practice? What's new and different about collaboration for 21st century learners?

The New Literacies for Collaboration

Studies on collaboration focusing on teacher practice overwhelmingly suggest that collaboration has a strong positive effect on instruction and student learning (Goddard, Goddard, & Tschannen-Moran, 2007; Schmoker, 2005). Collaboration now, however, has broadened to include connecting in digital space, adding a new dimension of possibilities and potential for our profession to become more accomplished. The revolution in technology has transformed how people find one another, interact, and collaborate to create knowledge. The digital era opens unprecedented opportunities to expand your traditional learning experience by participating in networked spaces where sharing and reciprocity are expected.

By shifting your mindset of what constitutes learning, you can seize the opportunity to interact with others in the global network and use communication technologies such as blogs, wikis, microblogging, social bookmarking, and social networking. At the same time, you bring what you learn in these networked spaces back to your conversations in your school- or district-based learning communities. You think and communicate globally to drive change and innovation locally. Or, as the authors of *The Power of Pull* propose, you move out to the edge where innovative thinking is a constant and bring what you learn back to the core (Hagel, Brown, & Davison, 2010).

This new mindset for learning affects what we need to know. With new technologies and cultural shifts, the traditional literacies and competencies that dealt with making sense of words, images, and other content on a printed page are no longer sufficient. The literacies required to be productive citizens in a media-rich world are more inclusive, meeting the complex demands of our times and evolving as technologies change (Collier, 2007). The self-evaluation rubric in figure 1.2 incorporates a number of models or frameworks related to emerging literacies with a particular emphasis on ISTE NETS standards for teachers (International Society for Technology in Education 2008). Organizations such as the National Council of Teachers of English (2007), the Metiri Group (n.d.), The Partnership for 21st Century Skills (2009), the International Society for Technology in Education (2008, 2009), the U.S. Department of Education (Atkins et al., 2010), and the MacArthur Foundation (Jenkins, 2006) all suggest that there is a new set of literacies that individuals need to master to be productive citizens in the 21st century. How do you measure up? Are you literate by today's standards? Are your students?

In the space provided next to each skill, enter a 0 through 4. Be sure to include a bulleted description (example) of each skill in action and link to an artifact when possible. Use the following scoring guidelines to determine your skill level for each section.

Scoring Guidelines

4 = Outstanding: Consistently, intentionally, advanced

3 = Great: Most of the time, purposefully, proficient

2 = Good: Inconsistent, planned, basic

1 = Fair: Introductory, spontaneous, limited

0 = Not at this time: Need training, need to investigate further, or need both

1. **Facilitate and inspire learning and creativity:** I can use my knowledge of subject matter, teaching and learning, and technology to facilitate experiences that advance learning, creativity, and innovation in both face-to-face and virtual environments. This includes student and teacher development of skills such as critical thinking and problem solving, communication and collaboration, and building relationships with others to pose and solve problems collaboratively and cross-culturally. I am also able to help learners develop literacies relevant to participatory culture such as play (the capacity to experiment with one's surroundings as a form of problem solving), performance (the ability to adopt

alternative identities for the purpose of improvisation and discovery), and simulation (the ability to interpret and construct dynamic models of real-world processes).

As a learner leader and teacher, I . . .

_____ Promote, support, and model creative and innovative thinking and inventiveness
Example:

_____ Engage learners as participants in exploring real-world issues and solving authentic problems using digital tools, global learning spaces, and resources
Example:

_____ Promote reflection using collaborative tools to reveal and clarify learners' conceptual understanding and thinking, planning, and creative processes, such as the ability to create, critique, analyze, and evaluate multimedia texts
Example:

_____ Model collaborative knowledge construction by engaging in learning with students, colleagues, and others in face-to-face and virtual environments
Example:

_____ **Total composite score for facilitating and inspiring learning and creativity**

2. **Design and develop digital-age learning experiences and assessments:** I can design, develop, and evaluate authentic learning experiences and assessments incorporating contemporary tools and resources to maximize content learning in context and to develop the knowledge, skills, and attitudes for learning such as creativity, communication, and critical thinking. I am aware of and can teach contemporary issues such as global awareness, financial, economic, business and entrepreneurial literacy, civic literacy, health literacy, and environmental literacy. I also understand and can model the participatory skills of appropriation (the ability to meaningfully sample and remix media content) and distributed cognition (the ability to interact meaningfully with tools that expand mental capacities).

As a learner leader and teacher, I . . .

_____ Design or adapt relevant learning experiences that incorporate digital tools and resources to promote learning and creativity
Example:

_____ Develop technology-enriched learning environments that enable all learners to pursue their individual curiosities and become active participants in setting their own educational goals, managing their own learning, and assessing their own progress; I am intentionally developing and helping my learners develop a digital footprint.
Example:

_____ Customize and personalize learning activities to address diverse learning styles, working strategies, and abilities using digital tools and resources
Example:

_____ Provide learners with multiple and varied formative and summative assessments aligned with content and technology standards, and use resulting data to inform learning and teaching
Example:

Figure 1.2: Self-evaluation rubric for new literacies of the 21st century. continued →

_____ **Total composite score for designing and developing digital-age learning experiences and assessments**

3. **Model digital-age work and learning:** Connected learners exhibit knowledge, skills, and work processes representative of an innovative professional in a global and digital society. This includes proficiency with the tools of technology; the ability to manage, analyze, and synthesize multiple streams of simultaneous information; the ability to scan one's environment and shift focus as needed to salient details; skill in transmedia navigation (the ability to follow the flow of stories and information across multiple modalities); as well as evidence of the dispositions of flexibility and adaptability, initiative and self-direction, and productivity and accountability.

As a learner leader and teacher, I . . .

_____ Demonstrate fluency in technology systems and the transfer of current knowledge to new technologies and situations; I use 21st century tools in my own learning and leading.
Example:

_____ Collaborate with students, peers, parents, and community members using digital tools and resources to support student success and innovation; I also have a personal learning network that includes peers from around the globe.
Example:

_____ Communicate relevant information and ideas effectively to students, parents, and peers using a variety of digital-age media and formats
Example:

_____ Model and facilitate effective use of current and emerging digital tools to collaborate and locate, analyze, evaluate, and use information resources to support research and learning
Example:

_____ **Total composite score for modeling digital-age work and learning**

4. **Promote and model digital citizenship and responsibility:** Connected learners understand local and global societal issues and responsibilities in an evolving digital culture and exhibit legal and ethical behavior in their professional practices. They also attend to the ethical responsibilities these complex environments require. Connected learners are able to apply digital judgment (the ability to evaluate the reliability and credibility of different information sources).

As a learner leader and teacher, I . . .

_____ Advocate, model, and teach safe, legal, and ethical use of digital information and technology, including respect for copyright, intellectual property, and the appropriate documentation of sources; I understand Creative Commons licensure and know how to license my own work as well as help my students license theirs.
Example:

_____ Address the diverse needs of all learners by using learner-centered strategies and providing equitable access to appropriate digital tools and resources
Example:

_____ Promote and model digital etiquette and responsible social interactions related to the use of technology and information
Example:

_____ Develop and model cultural understanding and global awareness by engaging with colleagues and students of other cultures using digital-age communication and collaboration tools
Example:

_____ **Total composite score for promoting and modeling digital citizenship and responsibility**

5. **Engage in professional growth and leadership:** Connected learners continuously improve their professional practice, model lifelong learning, and exhibit leadership in their school and professional community by promoting and demonstrating the effective use of digital tools and resources. They understand how to network (the ability to search for, synthesize, and disseminate information); negotiate (the ability to travel across diverse communities, discerning and respecting multiple perspectives, and grasping and following alternative norms); and develop collective intelligence (the ability to pool knowledge and compare notes with others toward a common goal).

As a learner leader and teacher, I . . .

_____ Participate in local and global learning communities to explore creative applications of technology to improve learning; I understand how to build a personal learning network.
Example:

_____ Exhibit leadership by demonstrating a vision of technology infusion, participating in shared decision making and community building, and developing the leadership and technology skills of others
Example:

_____ Evaluate and transparently reflect on current research and professional practice on a regular basis to make effective use of existing and emerging digital tools and resources in support of learning
Example:

_____ Contribute to the effectiveness, vitality, and self-renewal of the teaching profession and of my school and community in both physical spaces and online; I understand the value of open leadership and connected learning communities.
Example:

_____ **Total composite score for engaging in professional growth and leadership**

Think About

Are you multiliterate? Of these literacies, which is most surprising to you? Which do you find least and most challenging?

The Connected Learner

Technology offers constant opportunities for self-directed and self-selected learning. Educators—through connections with each other, new research, and continually evolving content—have opportunities to interact, reflect, and focus without control by experts. That autonomy can generate far-reaching changes in teacher perspectives and school culture as educators begin to feel ownership of their own learning.

Connected learners develop networks and coconstruct knowledge from wherever they live. Connected learners collaborate online, use social media to interact with colleagues around the globe, engage in conversations in safe online spaces, and *bring what they learn online back to their classrooms, schools, and districts*, as we mentioned previously.

Within these connections and networks, the complexity of learning and teaching becomes more apparent, and educators deepen their understanding. As networks and available knowledge expand and grow, and educators make additional connections, a more accomplished global teacher practice evolves—a practice that continually focuses on maximizing student learning and staying current with knowledge about learning.

A new culture emerges as teachers shift away from a paradigm of isolation and closed doors. Connected learners share a deep commitment to understanding ideas related to teaching and learning. Conversations turn to topics of practice rather than to the staffroom complaints and rumors that too often occupy faculty members' time and energy. As educators grow into connected learners, they not only start to ask more critical questions of each other related to practice, but they also begin to actively listen and closely attend to varied perspectives that may help the community of learners move forward.

George Siemens, a researcher on learning at the University of Athabasca, describes the way we learn in networks as a form of knowledge exchange, a way of collecting and curating stories and ideas, a virtual wayfinding. By leveraging our online networks, educators solve problems through collective activities such as *crowdsourcing*, a way to leverage the wisdom of the crowd and its resources by querying various virtual venues (Siemens, 2005a). Each new activity helps create new vocabulary in order to have a common understanding of what is being learned.

For some, connected learning is a major shift in posture from expert to learner. This shift suggests that members are open to and accepting of new ideas, which means they are willing to receive constructive criticism from colleagues serving as critical friends—a change in culture that can result in cognitive dissonance for those just starting to shift.

The foundation for creating positive, lasting change in schools begins with understanding the possibilities inherent in small but powerful conversations about learning. Connected learning is learning through relationships. Connected learning is self-directed, interest-based learning from and with each other, through formal as well as informal activities, from sources outside as well as inside our situated practice. Connected learning helps educators realize the potential for professional learning and the pedagogical shifts afforded by current and emerging web technologies. Connected learning is understanding the power of collaborating and acting collectively. Connected learning is about big pictures and complex concepts. But mostly, connected learning is about building professional networks to help you, throughout your professional career, reflect deeply and prod others to do the same.

Succeeding as a Connected Learner

Unlike learning in face-to-face professional learning communities alone, connected learners develop a more generic set of values that help them negotiate learning with others in a variety of environments. Additionally, because the members of a specific community or network generally create norms and values, it helps to have a system of beliefs that is flexible and open to differing perspectives. The literature reveals many attributes and dispositions of contemporary learners that position them well to adapt to learning in a connected world (Downes et al., 2002; D. Hargreaves, 2004; Prensky, 2001). We find that the connected learner:

- Is a co-learner, co-creator, and co-leader
- Is self-directed
- Is open-minded
- Is transparent in thinking
- Is dedicated to the ongoing development of expertise
- Commits to deep reflection
- Engages in inquiry
- Values and engages in a culture of collegiality
- Shares and contributes
- Commits to understanding gained by listening and asking good questions
- Explores ideas and concepts, rethinks, revises, and continuously repacks and unpacks, resisting urges to finish prematurely
- Exhibits the courage and initiative to engage in discussions on difficult topics
- Engages in strengths-based appreciative approaches
- Demonstrates mindfulness
- Displays a willingness to experiment with new strategies

A Day in the Life of a Connected Educator

How might a day in your life as a connected educator unfold? This scenario offers an example.

As the sun rises on the East Coast, Susan, an elementary teacher, checks Twitter to briefly connect with Robert, whom she has never met. He is a fourth-grade teacher in another country whose class is collaborating with hers on an environmental project. After verifying that she and Robert both feel it's the right time to move into the project's next stage, she turns to someone else in her personal learning network who has just tweeted a link to an article on a current educational policy debate in which she is interested. She retweets that link to her own Twitter followers, sharing what she feels is a good resource, and then saves it on Diigo (www.diigo.com), her social bookmarking tool. Diigo makes it simple to include some initial personal annotations while also noting comments of others who've read the text before her. She appends her "must come back to" tag to remind herself to read it more fully later.

Next, Susan turns to her RSS feed, which she manages with the free Google Reader tool (www.reader.google.com). Reader allows her to scan new material her students have posted to their blogs. In addition, she can see changes students have made to the class wiki and any comments and resources her team of teaching colleagues have posted for the next unit they will design together. Susan makes a note to reply with her revisions and ideas after the school day is over.

It's time for school to begin. In one class, Susan works with a group of fifth graders currently immersed in learning about Iceland's geology. One member of her personal learning network lives in Iceland and has arranged a live video chat with her class using the free Skype (www.skype.com) service. Susan's students are excited as they look over a mind map they've created online about the geography and science they want to learn. They brainstorm questions to ask their Icelandic experts. During the Skype session, the teachers and students in the United States and Iceland document the event by snapping photos with their smartphones and making personal, short video recordings to use later in their blogs.

Just before lunch, several students upload images to Susan's school Flickr (www.flickr.com) photo-sharing account. The class has opted to use a Creative Commons license that allows them to share the photos, in case the students in Iceland want to use the photos on their online sites as well. While the kids eat lunch, Susan spies a photo that displays real engagement. She adds a favorite relevant quote and uses tags to add the artifact to a growing pool of images on education and change.

In another class later in the day, Susan introduces a learning strategy she's read about in one of the global online communities of practice of which she's a member. She smiles as it plays out exactly as she hoped, pulling in contributions from one student she's been working hard to engage. She makes a mental note to send a thank-you e-card to the educator in Australia who suggested the idea—and quickly sends a direct Twitter message to her principal, letting her know how successful the event was and inviting her to stop by for a classroom visit.

After school, Susan revisits the online community and posts a reflection about using the new strategy, asking members for feedback on the remix (adjustment) she made to increase its effectiveness with her particular students. At the nudging of a colleague in her school learning community, she decides to also cross post the reflection on a social networking site they both frequent that focuses on pedagogy. Within minutes, she sees that three people from around the world have posted replies to her questions.

Before turning in for the night, Susan checks Facebook (www.facebook.com), where she has recently joined a group working to have an impact on education policy. A quick scan of the Save Our Schools and Education Week Facebook groups compels her to add her own thoughts to a discussion about how to move forward. Next, she links her post about the learning strategy she used in class today to her profile page and shares a few of the Iceland photos with her Facebook friends. There's time for a quick instant chat with her sister, who also is on Facebook. Then, even though her favorite television show is starting, Susan takes time to post a short reflection to her personal blog about the Skype conference. She remembers to add her thoughts to her learning team wiki and settles back for an hour of old-fashioned television drama.

This is what a connected learner's day might look like: coaching, sharing, connecting, collaborating, and leveraging her web of networks to improve personal practice and make schools more effective and exciting places.

Where Are We?

- The world is changing.

- Emerging technologies make it easier than ever to connect, collaborate, and learn together with others around the world.

- As connected learners, we must look at differences between cooperation and collaboration.

- Conversations that shift us from expert to learner are valuable.

- Twenty-first century learners must embrace new literacies to remain relevant in the current classroom environment.

Think About

We've described how we think about the connected educator. Take a moment to reflect on your understanding. How are our perspectives alike? How are they different?

Where to Now?

Only through reculturing—changing the values, dispositions, and beliefs we have about the purposes of school—will we be able to shift teaching and learning to a higher level. As Hayes Mizell notes, "The more often educators are engaged with their peers in effective professional learning, the more likely they will learn and the more likely it is their practice will improve" (2007, p. 2). To adapt to today's culture of fast-paced change, we need to become connected learners and own new literacies so we can bring student learning into the 21st century. Chapter 2 explores how connected learners bring together existing and new practices to create connected learning communities that shift learning to a higher level.

Get Connected

This book is an interactive professional development experience. Each chapter ends with an application that can help you build skills as a connected learner. By immediately applying what you learn, you will add to your learning network and increase your understanding of how to learn in a connected world. Two applications, Map Yourself and Tag It, will get you started.

Map Yourself

This first application will help all of us involved with this book connect. The URL takes you to a Google map, where we all will insert our locations and a brief description of our interests. You will need a Google or Gmail account. Begin by creating or logging in to your account.

Please type this URL into your web browser: http://bit.ly/dge7M7. Now follow these steps to add yourself to *The Connected Educator* map. (Visit **go.solution -tree.com/technology** for live links to the materials mentioned in this book.)

Step 1: Click on the Edit button at the top left. You will be able to see the Edit button only if you are logged in with your Google or Gmail account.

Step 2: Use the + and − tool to zoom in or out and find your location. Use the compass rose to move north, south, east, or west. Tools are in the upper left-hand corner of the map.

Step 3: Click on the blue "Add a placemark" pin symbol at the top of the map.

Step 4: Drag it to your location and click on your city or town.

Step 5: Edit the Place Information box by adding your name and a description. Click on OK.

Step 6: Save your changes.

Step 7: Click on Done in the left-hand column of the screen.

Your name should appear in the list in the left-hand column.

Tag It

The second application piece for this chapter relates to collectively developing a common language. Using the social web tool Diigo (http://diigo.com), we've created a common *tag* (an organizing word, phrase, or group of letters or numbers) that will, through the power of RSS web syndication, pull all our bookmarked web links to one place online. Wikipedia explains Diigo this way:

> **Diigo** (pronounced /ˈdiːgoʊ/) is a social bookmarking website which allows signed-up users to bookmark and tag webpages. Additionally, it allows users to highlight any part of a webpage and attach sticky notes to specific highlights or to a whole page. These annotations can be kept private, shared with a group within Diigo, or [via] a special link forwarded to someone else. The name "Diigo" is an abbreviation for "Digest of Internet Information, Groups and Other stuff." (Diigo, 2011)

After creating a Diigo account, find a few resources that help explain some of the concepts, terms, or ideas represented in this chapter, and label them with the general tag we've created to identify materials associated with this book: *clc-voc*. As readers begin to follow this practice, we will collectively create a dynamic resource that has the potential to deepen everyone's understanding of connected learning. Diigo can also help us connect to each other and to additional resources we have collected and vetted about other topics of interest.

Type the Diigo URL link into your web browser (www.diigo.com), and follow these steps to start tagging items for our collective concepts and definitions list.

1. Create a Diigo account if you do not have one. Visit http://bit.ly/4GsTJI for a tutorial for creating a Diigo Educator account.

2. Now watch this video tutorial on bookmarking (http://bit.ly/1WMILy), and add the Diigo toolbar to your browser.

3. Following the instructions in the tutorial, bookmark a website or resource that helps develop our common language and understanding for this chapter. Be sure to use the *clc-voc* tag, along with any others that will help you sort and retrieve the material later.

4. To view all the tags others are adding, type *http://diigo.com/tag/clc-voc* into your browser.

5. Explore Diigo, and add other users to your network. Here's a good way to add potential colleagues who are also reading this book:

- Go to http://diigo.com/tools

- Type *clc-voc* into the search box on the right and pick "search community library for *clc-voc*" from the drop-down menu that appears.

- You will see a list of links with badges next to each displaying the number of people that have bookmarked that link. The badge will say something like "12 people" or "288 people."

- Under the text describing the link, you will see "First saved by: [user]." Click on that user's name. That is the person who bookmarked that page on Diigo.

- Glance at that user's bookmarks. If that person consistently saves bookmarks that you find useful, click on the Follow Me button near the top right of the page.

- Return to that list of popular links, and add users who first found other pages.

- To see links from your network, click on your name at the top of Diigo, and select *Friends* from the drop-down menu.

Chapter Two

Developing a Connected Learning Model

Teacher collegiality and collaboration are not merely important for the improvement of morale and teacher satisfaction … but are absolutely necessary if we wish teaching to be of the highest order.

—L. S. Shulman, former professor of education, Stanford University

Our Stories

Two thousand learners in one course—can you even imagine? In 2008, two thousand learners participated in an open online course (Connectivism and Connective Knowledge), connecting as they sought to understand this new learning theory for the digital age. The tools made it possible for each of us to become autonomous learners in this new environment. The course design offered a variety of options to learn through The Daily (an email distribution list), a wiki, Moodle discussion forums, Elluminate sessions, Second Life meet-ups, blogs, RSS to pull feeds of learner blogs, Twitter, Netvibes, Skype, and Flickr. The tools enabled learners from all over the world to connect and collaborate.

My connections with course colleagues in Israel, the United Kingdom, Australia, New Zealand, Finland, Canada, and the United States left indelible path markers on my trail to deepened understanding. As I worked to synthesize their thoughts and mine, an unexpected synergy surged from my fingers to my keyboard and into the lines of my blog posts. My learning gained an entirely new dimension, thanks to the human connections the tools enabled.

Tentative, not always confident—

Enthusiastic, seeking those aha moments that arise from connecting with creative, smart, and innovative educators—

Hesitant, at times unsure—

Stretching, moving out of my comfort zone as I find my way. It's messy, it's formidable, and it's stupefying—21st century learning at its best! Learning that brings new meaning to being open to new ideas, to flexibility, to being nimble—challenging and demanding. Therein, for me, lies the pull—an ongoing wayfinding and self-directed learning through connecting.

—Lani

Traditionally, teacher professional learning has focused on acquiring new knowledge and skills through passive, system-sponsored workshops delivered on in-service days. In these workshops, teachers learn new pedagogy from an outside expert and then are expected to take the learning back to their classrooms and try it out. After the workshop, when daily routines and pressures take over, and teachers have no one to help them problem solve, they go back to business as usual. Bringing new strategies from theory into individual classroom practice is even more difficult when teachers try to implement innovation and change, since traditional professional development rarely offers ways for teachers to work together through the issues that emerge in practice.

In the traditional and still fairly typical teacher network, teachers' primary interactions are with family, local community, and colleagues we work with or meet face-to-face in professional settings. These interactive communications are most often disconnected from other inputs—mass media, curriculum documents, reports, handouts from professional development workshops, or digital information found on the web. In the absence of dynamic connectedness, those inputs are more likely to serve as a ballast for the status quo than fuel for positive change.

Our model of teacher networking doesn't replace the traditional network—it subsumes and transforms it. The connected teacher benefits from this traditional network and also has access to a much wider community that contains the knowledge of thousands of people, all connected to one another through technology (see figure 2.1).

Connected Learning Communities

Professional learning communities are valuable, but alone, they are not enough. We believe that a new model of professional development for the 21st century educator is necessary. This new model builds on the rich research and foundational concepts of traditional professional learning communities. What's different is how it transforms the teacher's traditional network by building community offline and *online*, leveraging emerging technologies in building personal learning networks and global communities of inquiry. Meet the new model for professional development: *connected learning communities*.

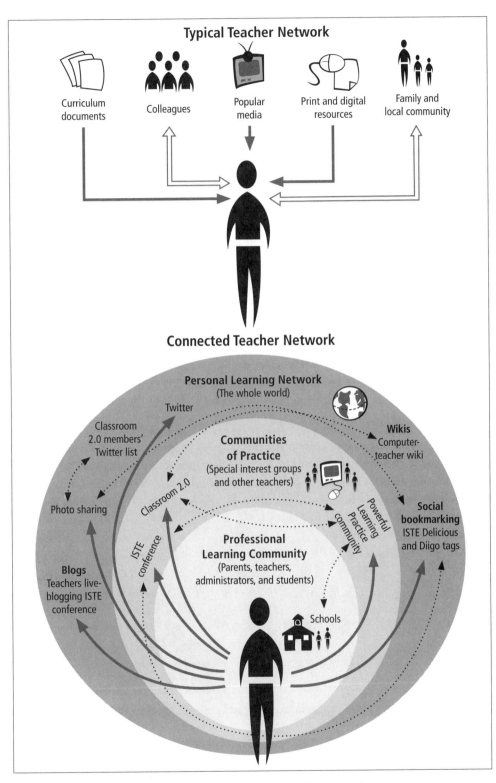

Figure 2.1: Typical teacher network versus connected teacher network.

Source: Typical Teacher Network used with permission from Alec Couros.

In connected learning communities, educators have several ways to connect and collaborate, in particular through *professional learning communities*, *personal learning networks*, and *communities of practice* or *inquiry* (see figure 2.2). In connected learning communities, colleagues develop shared visions, common goals, and beliefs around principled change. They brainstorm and talk about creative ways to meet the needs of the 21st century learner, and they devise strategies to motivate schools to transform learning environments, *thus ensuring their own sustainability* by becoming highly relevant in students' lives.

The connected learning community model advances a three-pronged approach to professional development.

1. **Local community:** Purposeful, face-to-face connections among members of a committed group—a *professional learning community* (PLC)

2. **Global network:** Individually chosen, online connections with a diverse collection of people and resources from around the world—a *personal learning network* (PLN)

3. **Bounded community:** A committed, collective, and often global group of individuals who have overlapping interests and recognize a need for connections that go deeper than the personal learning network or the professional learning community can provide—a *community of practice or inquiry* (CoP)

Professional learning communities (face-to-face) take a team focus, personal learning networks (online) take an individual focus, and communities of practice (face-to-face or online) take a systemic focus. It takes all three to provide the do-it-yourself, 21st-century teacher learner with the experiences needed to become effective in today's fast-changing world.

Figure 2.2: Connected learning communities—A three-pronged approach.

A Common Language

Many of the words and expressions used to describe learning in connected, open spaces are overused, used incorrectly, or used interchangeably. We believe it's important to arrive at a common language. A shared vocabulary will help the reader understand the unique traits and roles of several connected learning strategies we will examine closely in this book.

While we cannot solve the language issues in education as a whole, a shared vocabulary for these three interrelated learning strategies will help you understand the connected learning community approach. You also can refer to the glossary (page 147) when you are unsure of a term.

A quick survey of the literature on professional learning communities makes it obvious that *professional learning community* is a trendy term, one used interchangeably with other often-misunderstood terms such as *learning team*, *learning network*, *community of practice*, and more recently, *personal learning network* and *networked learning communities*. In fact, these terms have become so commonplace and have been used in conjunction with one another so often that they have lost much of their meaning.

Following are our definitions of the three key components of our connected learning communities model.

Professional Learning Communities

Professional learning communities, as we've discussed, are traditional school-based structures in which staff—both teachers and administrators—learn together with the goal of improving student achievement. This goal is seen as the responsibility of all educators in the school.

Professional learning communities are about continuous improvement, shared leadership, and school reform. High-functioning professional learning communities engage in collective and continuous inquiry, participate in thoughtful conversations about their professional learning, devise strategies to improve instruction, act on what they have created, and reflect together.

In professional learning communities, leadership is distributed, colleagues commonly visit classrooms to offer feedback, and members share a vision and support the group's activities (Hord, 1997). The shared decision-making characteristic of professional learning communities has been cited as an important component of school reform.

The organizational structures of professional learning communities (time to meet, flexible schedules to visit classrooms, support for action research) empower educators and encourage risk taking, and they can transform beliefs about an educator's role in school success. As Hall and Hord (1987) and Fullan (1993, 1994) note, individual learning is the road to systemic change. Professional learning communities encourage and capitalize on individual learning, fostering each educator's sense of self-efficacy as the team sets common goals. Teachers develop meaningful relationships that sustain them when they are faced with difficult issues (DuFour, DuFour, Eaker, & Many, 2006a). With a sense of empowerment, educators take ownership of the vision, mission, and shared responsibility for student learning (Hord, 1997).

In addition, the democratic practices found in professional learning communities can transform a school culture to one of collegiality and learning. A professional learning community can help teachers create and sustain a climate of inquiry throughout a school. As teachers collaborate to improve instruction and lead students to higher achievement levels, they begin to focus on inquiry. Best of all, when educators model inquiry, civil discourse, and continuous improvement, their actions have a positive impact on student engagement and student attitudes toward learning.

Professional learning communities can employ a range of web-based technology tools to connect, collaborate, work collegially, and reflect while immersing members in inquiry-based learning. With regular opportunities to discover the learning potential of blogs, wikis, and other collaboration and networking tools, participants begin to own these technologies and techniques and then to transfer their learning to professional practice. These tools help members document and share what the professional learning community is learning. The tools help the group create a digital footprint for the school, showing their growth and understanding.

Participating in a professional learning community is an important step in becoming a connected educator.

Putting It in Practice—Professional Learning Communities

Bill Ferriter, a sixth-grade language arts teacher from North Carolina, became an evangelist for professional learning communities following an aha moment when his team strongly encouraged him to incorporate Paideia principles and practices—a model of classroom discussion that references the Socratic method—into his repertoire of strategies for classroom instruction. In a post, he relates his PLC and classroom experience, concluding:

> Professional learning communities are different. Teachers agree to work together to examine and to reflect, collaborating in ways that are often foreign in our profession.

> The focus of teacher learning teams is on identifying what works for students. Shared knowledge is valued above all, and teachers have to be willing to open their practices to review and revision.

> *This collaboration leads to growth and to change—even in those of us who know that we're right—and holds great power to reform what happens in our schools. (Ferriter, 2010)*

Personal Learning Networks

While professional learning communities are about working collectively in grade-level, department-level, or schoolwide teams around common tasks related to student achievement, personal learning networks are about individuals gathering information and sharing resources that enhance their personal and professional learning. The primary difference between personal learning networks and professional learning communities is that the work of professional learning communities is designed around the specific, identified needs of the school and its students while personal learning networks are something that educators *design for themselves* to further their short- and long-range goals for professional growth and personal learning. While each can benefit the other, they are distinctly different.

Personal learning networks are a reciprocal learning system in which educators participate by sharing and then learning from others who share with them. Personal learning networks are *personal* in the sense that each of us selects our own set of connections as we pursue self-directed, independent learning experiences. Educators have always added to their storehouse of knowledge and skills through personal networks of colleagues who share particular interests. In the past, those networks were seldom large, their size determined by physical location and contact at professional conferences.

In our model of professional learning, a personal learning network comprises the connections educators make to extend learning and the environments or virtual spaces they create to engage colleagues or mentors. The availability of web-based technologies that promote connectivity has erased physical boundaries. Educators learn as they leave the confines of their classrooms and build a classroom and curriculum of their own around ideas they are passionate about, irrespective of physical space. The potential to establish regular communication with individuals and groups that share our interests from around the globe is virtually unlimited. When we leverage that capacity to connect to accelerate our own growth, we are building a personal learning network.

Growing and nurturing a personal learning network is a complex process. Educators must master digital tools and select trustworthy sources—individuals, resources, and organizations—in a safe, effective, and ethical way. Personal learning networks, though, have the potential to profoundly affect both professional and personal learning. The transformation in professional practice has significant ripple effects as the practitioner then models networking skills to students, helping them select, vet, and develop their own personal learning networks around their interests.

Putting It in Practice—Personal Learning Networks

Kathy Cassidy is a first-grade teacher in Moose Jaw, Saskatchewan, Canada, who uses technology to help her students connect, collaborate, and learn with people from around the world. She said of her personal learning network:

> Through online contacts such as my RSS feeds and Twitter (well, sometimes), I am exposed to the thoughts and ideas of people who are really thinking about education and change in a way that I never would without their prompting. They daily challenge my opinion and help me to be a better teacher. I am a "how-to" thinker and, like most primary teachers, including those in my school-based PLC, I think in practicalities rather than in big ideas. My online network allows me to be exposed to those ideas and thinking about how I can use them. (Cassidy, 2008)

Networking can help boost your energy, stimulate personal growth, and lead to a revitalized individual practice. Self-organized networks also can offer opportunities to join or create powerhouse communities of inquiry and practice—easily distinguishable from traditional networks by their deeper levels of thinking, collaboration, and engagement. Teachers and administrators working to advance their practices need both professional learning communities and personal learning networks. Personal learning networks are the do-it-yourself piece for the 21st century professional development menu.

Connectivism: A New Learning Theory

The type of learning that occurs in personal learning networks implies a shift—to greater transparency and self-directed, do-it-yourself learning. Through openly and transparently sharing ideas and artifacts, along with collaboratively constructing new knowledge, learners make connections and form relationships.

George Siemens (2005b, 2006) asserts, in his much-discussed article "Connectivism: A Learning Theory for the Digital Age" and his subsequent book *Knowing Knowledge*, that previous learning theories fail to explain how people learn when current technologies are taken into consideration. Instead of behaviorism, cognitivism, or constructivism, Siemens proposes *connectivism*, a framework of learning that makes sense of how information is connected in our world of constant change.

Connectivism gives us the language and the theoretical framework to describe the connected learner's process for learning. Traditionally, teacher learning has focused on the acquisition of new knowledge and skills, often through isolated, short-term workshops or presentations limited in collaboration and autonomous learning experiences. A connectivist view of teacher (and student) learning implies a shift to significant openness and collaboration, with constant opportunities for distributed, self-directed, and self-selected learning through the affordances of current technology. That autonomy can generate far-reaching changes in teacher perspectives and school culture as educators begin to feel a sense of ownership for their own learning. In connectivism, those engaged in the learning process construct learning collaboratively. They derive competence from forming connections. Stephen Downes, a Canadian researcher like Siemens, adds that we grow in connected ways when we engage online in practices to learn (Downes, 2007a).

Putting It in Practice—Connectivism

Ken Carroll lived and worked in Shanghai, China, between 1994 and 2009, where he coestablished a number of successful entities in the field of training and learning, including ChinesePod (http://chinesepod.com). While taking a course on connectivism (http://ltc.umanitoba.ca/wiki/Connectivism), he wrote a blog post on the ways he saw his work at ChinesePod squaring with the theory of connectivist learning. Here is an excerpt from that post:

> *The teachers and practitioners on ChinesePod do not see ourselves as lecturers or teachers who impart knowledge in the old sense. Instead, we are connectors, or resources who point learners at key patterns or elements that help strengthen their connection to a piece of information (and emphasize the skill of being able to identify patterns). (Carroll, 2008)*

Communities of Practice

Communities of practice (or inquiry) are *systems of collective critical inquiry and reflection* focused on building a shared identity and a collective intelligence garnered over time. Members have a "none of us is as good as all of us" mentality.

According to cognitive anthropologist Etienne Wenger (1998), communities of practice have three distinct criteria: (1) a shared domain of interest, (2) collective competence among equals who are skillful and talented, and (3) a shared practice or a common sense of purpose. Members of a community of practice are situated *practitioners.*

Communities of practice are made up of people with a common interest, who collaborate to learn to do it better. They may be a group of Paleo diet enthusiasts experimenting with eliminating grains from recipes without reducing taste, programmers working on an open-source computer application, nurses seeking to reduce error in hospitals, or educators working to promote writing across the curriculum.

Wenger says that "a community of practice is a group made up of like-minded individuals who share an interest, a concern, a set of problems, or a passion about a topic, and who deepen their knowledge and expertise in this area by interacting on an ongoing basis" (Wenger, McDermott, & Snyder, 2002, p. 4). The key to success in such communities is sharing information, learning, and developing opportunities.

For our purpose, these practitioners are situated in *an online, global, and diverse community*. They develop meaningful relationships with people they might never have met if not through the online community; they trust each other to interact, share, and co-create knowledge and content. Developing relationships in the community over time is important and cannot be rushed. Time creates a sense of trust that enables participants to share freely. Participants become more comfortable about constructing meaning and understanding in authentic ways.

Trust, empathy, and reciprocity are the glue for relationships that bond members together in any community or social setting, but even more so online (Preece, 2004), where they enable the flow of the knowledge sharing needed to solve problems, achieve shared goals, and sustain work. Through the collective wisdom and strong relationships within communities, members often make a courageous commitment to challenge the status quo.

In addition, members of a community of practice are practitioners who develop a common repertoire of resources and experiences around a shared practice. These online communities depart from the traditional view of learning, often explored in professional learning communities, that emphasizes individual knowledge and performance. Communities of practice often reject the expectation that teachers (or students) will acquire the same body of knowledge at the same time.

A driving force behind a community of practice is community knowledge, in which the sum of the collective knowledge is greater than the sum of the individuals' knowledge (Gherardi & Nicolini, 2002). As collective knowledge grows stronger, so does the individual's knowledge (Bielaczyc & Collins, 1999). This model holds the potential to push beyond the incremental culture of change to remake student and teacher learning experiences in ways that lead to exponential improvement and dramatic results. Communities of practice move beyond tasks and data interpretation, which typically occur in professional learning communities, to deep knowledge construction, innovation, and global citizenship.

Technological tools have made the world smaller while expanding the idea of community. Knowledge construction rarely is done in isolation these days. A burgeoning body of research suggests that virtual learning communities are becoming the venue through which change agents operate (Barab & Duffy, 2000; Dede, 2003; Johnson, 2001; Palloff & Pratt, 1999). New electronic models of professional growth inspire educators to collaborate differently, using innovative ways to share knowledge and advocate for educational reform. The potential is enormous as knowledge capital is collected and the community becomes a sort of online brain trust.

Communities of practice encourage collective reflection within a shared, situated context. Communities of practice have the goal of collective action through mobilizing the collective knowledge and social fabric of the online community to improve practice and create possibility. Educators who commit to learning together over time within a community of practice become empowered, global citizens. The importance of communities of practice is in the depth of members' reflection and inquiry and how they operationalize that co-created knowledge in their local, school-based learning community.

Putting It in Practice—Connected Learning

Rodd Lucier, a teacher in Ontario, Canada, who is part of Sheryl's Twitter network, describes a connected educator in a way that resounds with us: "When no 'one' you know knows, a connected educator knows that nodes know" (Lucier, 2010). George Siemens describes nodes in this way: "Regardless of name, a node is any element that can be connected to any other element. A connection is any type of link between nodes" (2005a). So, in a connected space, we each become nodes, part of a huge network of learning options.

Table 2.1 summarizes the three prongs of connected learning communities in regard to the method, purpose, structure, and focus of each.

Table 2.1: The Three Prongs of Connected Learning Communities

	Professional Learning Communities	Personal Learning Networks	Communities of Practice
Method	Often organized *for* teachers	Do-it-yourself	Educators organize it themselves
Purpose	To collaborate in grade-level or subject-area teams around tasks	For individuals to gather information for personal knowledge construction or to bring back to the professional learning community	Collective knowledge building around shared interests and goals
Structure	Team or group or face-to-face	Individual, face-to-face, and online	Collective, face-to-face, or online
Focus	Student achievement	Personal growth	Systemic improvement

The Research Behind Our Model

Decades of research and scholarship support our *connected learning communities* model. Networked learning is not a recent phenomenon triggered by advances in technology. Networking and collaboration in education have a long, rich history. Considerable research on local learning communities has highlighted the benefits of networked collaboration for connected learning in the digital age. The bulk of the literature focuses on professional learning communities, but it also addresses communities of practice and personal learning networks. Diverse studies often focus on processes and persistently find a positive shift in both educators' professional learning and in student learning *when educators invest time in collaboration and reflection.*

Linda Darling-Hammond and her colleagues note that "teachers need to learn the way other professionals do: continually, collaboratively and on the job" (Darling-Hammond, Wei, Andree, Richardson, & Orphanos, 2009, p. 1). In the coauthored report, *Professional Learning in the Learning Profession*, Darling-Hammond and her colleagues find that collaborative professional learning teams lead to growth of personal teaching practice and student achievement. Yet the report also notes that isolation is a serious issue, with teachers reporting little collaboration. In a 2009 research review for *Educational Leadership*, Darling-Hammond and Nikole Richardson conclude that "professional learning communities can change practice and transform student learning—when they have in place the processes and structures that make true joint work possible and desirable" (Darling-Hammond & Richardson, 2009, p. 50).

Cochran-Smith and Lytle (1993) describe a knowledge base for teaching based on collaboration and action research. They propose a dramatic shift in viewing not only how teachers learn but also teachers' roles in developing their own knowledge base. They propose that teachers move from users and subjects to *knowers and participants.* They see the co-creation of a knowledge base occurring through collaborative communities of teacher researchers.

Researchers have found that instructional capacity is improved when professional development for educators is ongoing, embedded within the context of particular learning situations, and based on collaborative, inquiry-based learning (Knapp, McCaffrey, & Swanson, 2003; Senge, 1990a). These are all attributes of high-functioning learning communities. Furthermore, learning communities adopt a systemic approach that helps address a randomness of quality that can characterize individual practice. When teachers become active members of collaborative teams, they work interdependently on common goals and hold each other mutually accountable. The team members, using evidence of student learning, assist each other with an awareness of student strengths and weaknesses. Members are persuaded to embrace more effective instructional practices by improved student results.

In addition, when teachers collaborate and share their practices collaboratively, they become aware of colleagues with better results and are more receptive to adopting effective practices that lead to improved teaching and learning (DuFour, 2009).

In studies of school effectiveness, those forms of collaboration and collegiality that incorporate factors such as shared decision making, distributed leadership, and openness around practice correlate to improved school effectiveness and student achievement (Copland, 2003; Harris, 2004; Leithwood, Steinbach, & Jantzi, 2002). Collaboration and collegiality are the glue that holds teacher development, motivation, and meaningful change together as schools shift away from mandated accountability to mutual accountability and acknowledge school improvement as a component of their professional obligation.

The U.S. Department of Education has seen value in also shifting to a more global and connected view of education, as outlined in *Transforming American Education: Learning Powered by Technology*, a National Education Technology Plan released in November 2010 (Atkins et al.). The plan calls for applying the technologies we use in our daily personal and professional lives to education in order to improve student learning, accelerate and scale up the adoption of effective practices, and use data for continuous improvement.

The report states, "Professional educators will be supported individually and in teams by technology that connects them to data, content, resources, expertise, and learning experiences that can empower and inspire them to provide more effective teaching for all learners" (Atkins et al., 2010, p. 39). The plan suggests that "episodic and ineffective professional development" will be replaced by "professional learning that is collaborative, coherent, and continuous and that blends more effective in-person courses and workshops with the expanded opportunities, immediacy, and convenience enabled by online learning" (Atkins et al., 2010, p. 41). It goes on to say:

> Online learning communities break through educators' traditional isolation, enabling them to collaborate with their peers and leverage world-class experts to improve student learning. . . . Educators are no longer limited by where they teach or where they lead, nor are they required to deliver teaching as solo practitioners. (p. 42)

The report also notes, "The best way to prepare teachers for connected teaching is to have them experience it" (Atkins et al., 2010, p. 44).

The case for collaborative, connected professional learning is evidence based and is supported by research and our professional experiences working with more than four thousand educators worldwide through Powerful Learning Practice and other, large-scale, community-driven projects in Norway, Australia, New Zealand, Canada, and across the United States.

In conversations when we have asked teachers, "How has your learning changed because of being connected?" or "How has your classroom or leadership style changed?" we have heard responses such as, "Because I did so-and-so [some connected activity], it gave me the confidence and self-assurance to do this other thing [usually some significant change piece]." Frequently a breakthrough in collegial sharing in both face-to-face and online spaces occurs because of a willingness to take a risk and share transparently; from that sharing, learners become connected. How can connected learning communities lead to instructional improvement? Often, the confidence or self-efficacy developed online leads to a commitment to continuous improvement among and with colleagues in the local context.

We provide a more extensive understanding of the research behind elements of connected learning communities in appendix A (page 153).

Putting It in Practice—Connected Learning Communities

For Mary Rochford, superintendent of Catholic Schools for the Archdiocese of Philadelphia, the connection between learning together online and instructional improvement is obvious. "We are all in this together," she said. "We need to be better at connecting and collaborating. I am seeing the leaps the world is taking, and they are not minor leaps. We need to take advantage of opportunities, and bring our students in it, or we will find ourselves being left behind" (M. Rochford, personal communication, May 2, 2010).

What Connected Learning Communities Do

Connected learning communities, the new model of 21st century professional development, enable individual educators to create their own online learning networks of local and global colleagues. Technology allows us to create a virtual think tank of professional experts, students, parents, and many others, all learning forward as we determine what's best for children in this fast-changing world.

Connected learning communities are designed to support the professional development goals their members have chosen to improve instruction and subsequently bring about increased growth and achievement for the 21st century learner. Members of connected learning communities collaborate and work interdependently to achieve high levels of student achievement, while also focusing on their own professional and personal learning goals.

Because connected learning communities are built on the rich empirical foundation of what works in professional learning communities, personal learning networks, and communities of practice, their ability to achieve their purpose is strengthened by interactions and learning experiences taking place at many levels and in many contexts. Members of connected learning communities learn by making and developing connections (intentionally or not) between ideas, experiences, and information. They also learn by interacting, sharing, understanding, accepting, commenting, and creating—by defending their own opinions and viewpoints and reflecting on their current situations and daily experiences both in and out of the classroom (Aceto, Dondi, & Marzotto, 2010). Connected learning communities provide the context, resources, and opportunities to expand learning in

very transparent ways; participants gain not only self-awareness but also an awareness of those with whom they are connected. The unique blend of personal and
professional learning that occurs in connected learning communities increases
knowledge acquisition for educational practice and personal growth among individuals who feel seamlessly interwoven. Members find themselves not just learning how to be better educators but more tuned-in and effective people.

The willingness and commitment to explore ideas and concepts demands an
intellectual perseverance toward rethinking and revising conversations. We've
found that those educators who take part in online connections somehow find
and value the time to think deeply about ideas and strategies, to unpack them, and
to seriously consider how they inform practice in their classrooms and schools.
Knowledge construction in connected learning communities becomes a continual,
rigorous process—one in which learners persevere despite inclinations to declare,
"We are finished."

Putting It in Practice—In the Classroom

Patti Grayson is a third-grade teacher at Hampton Roads Academy in Virginia.
In a blog post, she shares just how tough receiving constructive criticism can
be to someone who is new to connected learning:

> *Most recently, our team has created and begun implementing our
> action research project, the culminating project for the year. It took
> an enormous amount of brainstorming, patience, and determination
> to create a project that would work for our entire Pre-K to 12 faculty.*

> *Our first idea was entirely too broad. When we presented it during
> an Elluminate session with our cohort, we got shot down—hard. We
> were angry, frustrated, and went back to our corner sulking and
> fuming . . . for a day. Then we took a deep breath, pulled together,
> and got down to business. (Grayson, 2011)*

The desire to be transparent in thinking can be particularly difficult for teachers
who have spent years in professional isolation, teaching behind closed doors with
few opportunities to share. Developing the willingness to be open, to articulate
in a public space about personal practice, to share strategies, perspectives, and
lessons learned—all this is hard for teachers who view their practice as unique or
lack confidence in what they have to offer. Yet it is from transparency—sharing
what worked and what didn't, our successes and our stumbling blocks—that we
develop a common commitment to improve student learning and assume collective responsibility for achieving it. When reluctant collaborators can witness other
teachers revealing the learning path they have followed, signaling the trust and
strong relationships already present in the connected community, the distrust and
fear begin to ebb, and teachers new to the community are far more likely to risk

stepping out of their own comfort zones. When I watch you share your journey, potholes and all, and I realize that you are learning as you go, I gain the confidence needed to take small steps outside my closed space. The new sense of freedom enables me to take more risks, especially when colleagues in the community celebrate and reinforce the risk taking.

All this points to the fact that the success of a connected learning community is built on members' willingness to create a trust-based community—to share, laugh, celebrate, push, and empathize with each other. As the connected learning community members tie professional reflection to classroom applications, each models and demonstrates for the others the various modes of thinking—"technological, situational, deliberate, and dialectical" (Grimmett, Erickson, Mackinnon, & Riecken, 1990, pp. 20–38)—that underlie reflection, and we collectively move beyond basics to a more systemic knowledge of practice.

Connected learning communities often arise from a common desire to talk about what is working or not working in classrooms, schools, and organizations—and how what works is changing. The best connected learning communities have strong visions and clarity of purpose—and often begin organically. Core leaders (whether teachers or principals or other change agents) almost always direct and lead them, and the connected educators in these connected learning communities feel empowered to take charge of their individual and collective professional growth. Skills such as critical thinking, active learning, problem solving, developing an online voice, and collaborative action research all are fostered through the connected relationships that build over time.

Collective Action

Communities are about collective action. Here are a few of the acts connected learning communities can do to deepen learning. Moving these to online, global communities allows for diverse perspectives and strengthens the experience.

Action research groups: Do active, collaborative research focused on improvement around a possibility or problem in a classroom, school, district, or state.

Book study groups: Collaboratively read and discuss a book in an online space.

Case studies: Analyze in detail specific situations and their relationship to current thinking and pedagogy. Write, discuss, and reflect on cases using a 21st century lens to produce collaborative reflection and improve practice.

Connected coaching: Assign a connected coach to individuals on teams who will discuss and share teaching practices in order to promote collegiality and help educators think about how the new literacies (discussed in chapter 1) inform current teaching practices. Connected coaches practice appreciative inquiry as a means of working from a place of strength.

Critical friends: Form a professional learning team consisting of approximately five to ten educators who come together voluntarily at least once a month. Have members commit to improving their practice through collaborative learning. Use protocols to examine each other's teaching or leadership activities and share both warm and cool feedback in respectful ways.

Curriculum review or mapping groups: Meet regularly in teams to review what team members are teaching, to reflect together on the impact of assumptions that underlie the curriculum, and to make collaborative decisions. Teams often study lesson plans together.

Instructional rounds: Adopt a process through which educators develop a shared practice of observing each other, analyzing learning and teaching from a research perspective, and sharing expertise.

The Need for Diversity

Connected learning communities are perfect greenhouses for nurturing innovation because learners are exposed to different ideas and cultures. Connected learners are part of a boundless and timeless do-it-yourself learning environment where people with diverse backgrounds, knowledge, location, language, religion, experience, and cultural values provide insights for new approaches to commonly shared interests and issues, including 21st century change in schools (Aceto et al., 2010). The global citizenship aspect of connected learning communities naturally brings together individuals who are united by the common thread of better practice on behalf of children, yet differ greatly in the way they see the world, in their experiences, in their skills and talents, and in the way they frame their thinking.

Michael Fullan suggests, "Successful organizations don't go with only like-minded innovators; they deliberately build in differences" (Fullan, 2001b, p. 43). By their very nature and design, connected learning communities are characterized by a culture of collaboration, collective inquiry into best practice, an awareness of learning by doing, a commitment to continuous improvement with a focus on results (DuFour et al., 2006a), and a diversity of experience and thought that can lead to innovative changes.

Successful learning communities evolve and mature, embracing diverse members who differ in what they bring to the community in terms of background, experience, and knowledge of practice. The importance of diversity is foundational for organizations and individuals wanting to reculture, transform, or totally reinvent themselves in order to remain relevant in students' lives. To stimulate new ideas, facts, experiences, possibilities, insights, perspectives, and skills—conceptions and conversations need to bump up against each other in fresh and surprising ways. It is almost impossible to have something new emerge from people who hang out together all the time and think about the same things in much the same ways.

One of the strengths in collaborating as connected learners, both within and beyond the schoolhouse walls, lies in the range of thought, ideology, and culture that becomes part of the conversations and learning process. Connected learners expand their schemas and process issues and possible solutions from new perspectives and conceptual frames. Connected learners are able to hear differing voices and opinions and learn to confront challenges to assumptions authentically, in the manner of critical friends.

Those who see themselves as learners first are more likely to learn from others who challenge our thinking than from those with whom we wholeheartedly agree. In our experience, members of connected learning communities see the three-word text message "I totally agree" as a waste of time and attention. We want to know why or why not—what's been our own experience, what's to be done. In a community in which conversation follows this kind of norm, learning happens.

The Power of Diversity

In 2006, Sheryl had a personal lesson in just how powerful diversity can be. She was present in a Skype (www.skype.com) chat room with twenty people, taking part in the culminating event of a new kind of online conference she cofounded. K12Online (http://k12onlineconference.org) is a free mix of practitioners' live and asynchronous events and presentations. Over three days, educators from all over the world shared in the mixed-media sessions about 21st century teaching and learning concepts.

Now it was 2 a.m., and Sheryl found herself contributing to a dynamic discussion among educators who attended the recent conference. When she was asked to repeat herself several times, she was puzzled. Was it some degradation of the Skype transmission? Why couldn't her new colleagues understand? When the moderator finally said, "It is your accent, we can't get past the accent," she quickly scanned the list of people in the room and realized she was the only American. "I was amazed and humbled," she recalled.

Her realization served as a wake-up call that *she* was the one with the accent; the diversity of the room meant she needed to slow down and think about the words she was using. In globally connected communities, we might not always be on the same sheet of music because of culture and geography. Sheryl quickly realized that to be understood, she would need to consider all perspectives and not just her American-centric one. It was a game changing moment for her.

Educators in connected learning communities make outreach a priority. They not only ask questions among themselves, but they venture out into the global network. They engage in powerful conversations with individuals in and out of education, and then pull what they have learned into the bounded space, where they cultivate joint action plans that produce greater student learning and better teaching practice.

By developing shared beliefs, visions, and dispositions, connected educators establish a fertile soil in which they learn how to better cultivate a safe environment that nurtures the whole child. Diversity is seen as a strength, not a weakness.

Where Are We?

- We use the term *connected learning communities* to describe a three-pronged approach (involving professional learning communities, personal learning networks, and communities of practice) to effective professional development in the 21st century.

- Diversity is important in a learning community.

- Transparency is often difficult, but it is a powerful learning strategy for connected educators.

- Using a common language is important when building a shared understanding and common purpose.

- Social learning through community, networks, and groups has a rich history and research base.

- When teachers collaborate, they work on common goals and hold each other mutually accountable.

Think About

What benefits can you imagine a diverse network would provide? What are some ways you can ensure that your network is made up of all sorts of different people of different ages, experience levels, and perspectives? Do you think having a diverse range of opinions (versus people who always agree with you) in your network would help you grow as a learner? How?

Where to Now?

In chapter 3, we ask you to explore with us our role as learners—that's right, learners—not teachers, not leaders. We look at education and professional learning through the lens of a learner. We ask you to delve into the world of inquiry and passion-based learning that we believe will reignite any fires that policy trends may have dampened. Let's look together at learning first, teaching second.

Get Connected

In this application piece, we will create a collaborative reflection on the case for connected learning using VoiceThread. A VoiceThread is a collaborative conversation around a topic. It can consist of images, video clips, sound recordings, and more. Visit http://voicethread.com/share/409, and watch the video to see how it works. Visit http://voicethread.com/support/howto/Basics to view the how-to section if you need help with VoiceThread.

1. Go to https://voicethread.com/register, and register for an account.

2. Visit http://voicethread.com/share/1640351, and leave a comment answering this question:

   - Our schools need to change. We need to make the classroom a place that is tailored to the way connected learners learn. Can we accomplish that through collaboration and community? Do you believe that to remain effective for today's learner, we must change the way we teach and the way we learn to provide time for deep conversations and reflection? Why or why not? And if so, how?

Chapter Three

Learning to Learn

Through learning we re-create ourselves.
Through learning we become able to do
something we were never able to do.

—Peter Senge, founding chair, the
Society for Organizational Learning,
Massachusetts Institute of Technology

Our Stories

Growing up in a house without many books or educational opportunities, I had always seen learning as something contrived, something that happened at school. My older sister, Debbie, was the first to ignite my passion for learning. As I watched her draw at the table, I longed to draw people with the lifelike characteristics hers had. I made her show me how to make my people look like hers, and I practiced until I had it down.

I remember lying awake at night, straining to hear the interesting conversations the adults were having. I wanted to know what they knew. Later, as I became passionate about early childhood education and parenting, Debbie showed me how to be a self-directed learner through books. Neither of us had enough money to buy books, nor did the local library have the ones I wanted, so Debbie copied whole books on a mimeograph machine and used another machine at her work to bind them. Later in life, I watched *Beauty and the Beast* and gasped when Beast presented Beauty with a library—swearing one day I would have one, too, with real, hardback books.

Today, I see myself as a hardcore learner before I am anything else. The difference between now and then is that information is so available, books are had with a few clicks, and interesting conversations abound, sometimes with those I have never met face-to-face. I am thankful that I live in a connected age.

—Sheryl

To meet the needs of the learners of today and tomorrow, we need to recreate ourselves. We need to rethink how we do our job. We need to redefine our actions as educators so that we are teaching students how to learn, in part by modeling the role of lead learner. We need to stop thinking of a teacher as the giver of all knowledge and students as passive receivers of all knowledge and adopt a learner-first attitude.

One way to become a learner first is by finding our inner Jason. Who is Jason? He is a four-year-old boy that Sheryl sat behind on a plane ride.

"Look, a water truck! Mom! Mommy, look a water truck!" the boy exclaimed, glued to the window. When Sheryl glanced out at the tarmac, she saw that the child was excitedly pointing to a fire truck. Thinking about his childish vernacular, she realized he was actually right. It *was* a water truck. It made perfect sense. Rather than defining the vehicle by the problem (fire), Jason defined the solution (spraying water to put out the fire) and our gifts (what we do well). We are what we do: Jason's water truck sprays water. It is a water truck first, a fire putter-outer second. Similarly, when we help children learn, we are making learning happen. Learning is what we do. We are learners first, teachers second.

As author and educational reformer John Holt says:

> The most important thing any teacher has to learn, not to be learned in any school of education I ever heard of, can be expressed in seven words: Learning is not the product of teaching. Learning is the product of the activity of learners. (John Holt, 2011)

Teaching does not make learning occur. Learners create learning. Taking on a new role, taking a posture of learning, means recreating ourselves and rethinking how we do our jobs. We stop looking at the fire and start looking at the water.

Constructing Knowledge

True learning, deep retention, and knowledge construction really have little to do with school or teaching. We learn because we want to, because it's important to us, because it's natural, and because it's impossible to live in the world and not learn. What Dewey taught us still holds true: "Education is a social process. Education is growth. Education is not a preparation for life; education is life itself" (Dewey, 1897, p. 78).

I Define Learning as . . .

This transcript of an online discussion from February 2011 Sheryl started shows just how powerful and organic knowledge construction can be among a community of educators who see themselves as learners first. Participants were asked to define what learning means to them. The chat is a deeper look into how transparent sharing as a learner leads to collaborative knowledge building.

Many responses build on the ideas before theirs, a phenomenon that we believe occurs more easily in text-based discussions.

Sheryl: "I define learning as . . ."

Katie Niven: "Being able to take the knowledge you acquire and apply it in new situations."

Debbie Parker: "Acquiring a new understanding of something."

Theresa: "An understanding of the concepts, not just knowledge of the facts."

Lauri Brady: "Constructing knowledge."

Heather Geist: "Learning is personal growth."

Matthew Witmer: "A transformation from not knowing, to knowing, to doing."

Phyllis Boyd: "An ongoing process that changes and builds."

Greg Frederick: "Being able to do something you couldn't do before."

jeanette: "I think of learning as based in a desire to know more. Inquiry."

Tim Butz: "Learning is problem solving."

Kelly: "Learning is connecting what you already know to something new and applying it to real life situations that are meaningful to you."

Lyn Hilt: "Learning is investing in an exploration of new ideas, concepts, and skills, evaluating their relevance to your life, and applying them to continue to build knowledge."

sherriwilliams1: "Increasing knowledge in a manner that is effective to the individual."

Pat McKeon: "Acquiring the necessary skill set through exploration and investigation to be able to solve your own problems and create new concepts, ideas and innovations."

Lyn Hilt: "Learning is personal."

Rebecca: "Learning is as different for students as teaching is for teachers."

Dennie Boltz: "Learning should NOT be memorization."

Teresa Fleming: "Learning is both a personal construct and collaborative construct."

The most inspirational moment in this collaborative discussion occurred as the discussion was winding down, when one community member took all of the chat responses and put them in a visualization tool called Wordle. Visit www .wordle.net/show/wrdl/3450347/What_is_Learning%3F to see the results. (Visit **go.solution-tree.com/technology** to see the Wordle and for links to the URLs mentioned in this book.)

Cochran-Smith and Lytle (1999) describe learning as the construction of knowledge. They explain that educators construct knowledge for, in, and of practice.

Knowledge for practice is often reflected in traditional professional development when a trainer shares information that educational researchers have produced. The users agree that the knowledge shared has been validated in research, is effective, and is worth knowing. This kind of "sit and get" experience typically involves passively learning the information. You could attend an in-service, participate in a book study, or perhaps read a book such as this one. But educators usually have a difficult time transferring knowledge learned this way to classrooms and schools without support and follow-through (which is why we hope you participate in the Get Connected sections at the end of each chapter). "Sit and get" experiences *should* be part of the knowledge acquisition phase of learning, especially for novices. *Knowledge for practice* lays the groundwork for gaining expertise and gives you something to share in networks and communities. However, in isolation, without the opportunity to apply the learning to teaching, gaining passive knowledge typically is not enough to produce needed shifts in practice.

Knowledge in practice recognizes the importance of educator experience and practical knowledge for improving practice. This is the "try it out and see if it works" phase of knowledge construction. As you test strategies and assimilate them into teaching and leadership routines, you construct *knowledge in practice*, learning through experience. Educators strengthen their knowledge by reflecting and sharing the tacit or hidden knowledge embedded in experience. To change your practice, you need *knowledge in practice* opportunities to share with others and receive feedback. Learning in this way develops your capacity to become a transparent learner, one who values the connected feedback of online networks and the school community. The key is tapping into your professional learning community and personal learning network and using them as sounding boards for *what works* and *what doesn't*. Your ability to construct knowledge in practice is strengthened by the quality of your connections beyond the school-based professional learning community.

Knowledge of practice suggests a systematic inquiry in which teachers and leaders collaboratively create new understandings as they raise questions about and systematically study their practices. This kind of inquiry allows for deep learning in ways that move beyond the basics of classroom practice. The focus shifts beyond just learning by doing to examine such questions as, How do we get better at what we do? How can we improve and not just add new knowledge? What innovations can grow from what we know? This systematic inquiry involves reflection, conversations, and focused action. It involves opportunities to mediate perceptions, values, beliefs, information, and assumptions through continuing conversations within a diverse, global learning community and then bringing what is learned back to the local context. Educators who are transparent learners need other transparent learners in order to learn most effectively. The building and refining of ideas through the three-pronged approach of connected learning communities produces the most enduring understanding. In connected learning communities, ideas are generated together and mediated together, and innovation grows from the emerging collective intelligence.

Putting It in Practice—In the Classroom

A team of teachers at Saint Anastasia School in Newtown Square, Pennsylvania, has been developing knowledge for, in, and of practice as they work to understand problem-based learning in the classroom. The team learned about problem-based learning first through passive listening and in conversations within their online community of practice from expert Kevin Honeycutt (*knowledge **for** practice*). Later with their students, they participated in *Doomsday 1* (http://plpnetwork.com/pbl.html), an online, problem-based learning practice experience designed to give teams the opportunity to try suggested strategies (*knowledge **in** practice*). The teachers gave their students a scenario in which they needed to save the world from a meteor on a crash course with Earth. The students and teachers became co-learners as they met with experts, brainstormed ideas, and got feedback from their professional learning communities and online community. Team members developed a final presentation (http://vimeo.com/21211425) showing the innovation they designed to address the impending doom. Next, they scaled their learning as they reflected with team members who hadn't gone through the practice *save the world* experience. They then designed their own problem-based learning unit based on the conversation and exploration (*knowledge **of** practice*), leveraging the knowledge they had developed across their global learning community.

You can visit http://plparchdiocese10.wikispaces.com/St.+Anastasia to learn more about their learning. The school team members became connected learners. The potential for authentic change in how we construct knowledge exists best when connected learners co-create reform. To become connected learners, we unlearn, co-learn, and take responsibility for our own learning.

Unlearning and Relearning

By developing knowledge for, in, and of practice, we enhance professional growth, which can lead to real change. Change requires all three types of knowledge. The perfect environment for achieving all three is in a connected learning community. Connected learning allows the learner to construct knowledge through passive (knowledge for), active (knowledge in), and reflective (knowledge of) strategies.

Connected learning is a process of learning, unlearning, and then relearning as we participate in networks and communities. A fast-changing world creates a need to unlearn tacit knowledge (Brown, 2001). Unlearning is necessary, although it is often difficult and painful because it involves grieving for what we leave behind.

Futurist Alvin Toffler says, "The illiterates of the 21st century will not be those who cannot read and write but those who cannot learn, unlearn, and relearn" (Toffler, 2011). Educators invest thousands of hours in what we know, in in-services, courses, and reading. Leaving all that behind costs us. However, in connected communities, we weigh colleagues' contributions against what we believe to be true, test ideas, and leave behind what no longer fits. To make sense of new learning, we relearn and construct new knowledge that improves practice.

Several basic concepts of the digital age require unlearning. We need to unlearn that learning occurs only in school, is limited by time and space, and is an individual pursuit. We need to unlearn the idea that we have to be experts in our classrooms and that leading is only for those with titles. Visit www.facebook.com /edutopia/posts/146746198731330 to see an organic conversation that connected learners had around *unlearning*.

Think About

What do you need to unlearn and relearn?

Co-Learning

After years of *talking head* professional development, years of *teacher-as-knowledge-giver* in the front of the room, and years of *mandated accountability*, the shift to being a co-learner in a community can be a stretch. Yet to collectively advance and transform schools, we must become co-learners. We can't construct knowledge in isolation. Through conversations and connections, we learn socially together (Lave & Wenger, 1991). None of us knows everything. The term *distributed cognition* refers to the fact that we each know bits and pieces.

Technology allows us to collaborate differently, in half the time, sharing and combining our knowledge and expertise, and advocating for educational reform. Learning in an open social network is different from learning in a closed community. As we make connections, we grow and enlarge our perspective and "construct, use, reconstruct, and reuse knowledge in continuous cycles" (Riel & Polin, 2004, p. 32). Knowledge, rather than being shared between learners, is *stretched across* community members (Waters & Gasson, 2007). Through asking questions, sharing similar and opposing points of view and experiences, and then negotiating meaning (Gunawardena, Lowe, & Anderson, 1997), we build a collective understanding of our practice. This process of co-learning begins when we are willing to see ourselves as learners first.

Putting It in Practice—In the Classroom

Lisa Snyder, the head of information services for The Haverford School in Haverford, Pennsylvania, comments on a discussion in her online community of practice:

Boy, they weren't kidding when they said this would be powerful! From the very first, I've done nothing but learn. I would admit, though, that a lot of what I've learned I had not expected to.

What I've come to realize is that, through our online community we are gaining exposure to the world that our kids already inhabit easily—and learning in that environment is not neat and tidy. I wrote my first Ning post about ambiguity and how learning to live—and learn—in an ambiguous world is not easy. It requires openness to new experiences and letting go of my tradition-based ideas of what schooling is. Learning is not linear, and while I've espoused that for years, it wasn't until this experience that I was able to live the non-linear, sometimes frustrating, always interesting world of a 21st Century learner.

I've also experienced the very powerful feeling that comes from having a colleague read my posts, find something in there of use, and respond in a thoughtful, serious way to my thoughts. Authentic assessment! Wow, I always knew it was an important concept, but I didn't know how it would feel to receive authentic feedback from people I respect and admire. It feels great!

So, the lessons I've learned have been important ones. For those who are wondering, What's next? or, When are we actually going to do something? I would have to argue that, if you really take a learning posture—give up your control and your need to feel industrious—you will find that you are learning. And you have been all along! (Fisch, 2008)

Taking Responsibility

Connected learners take responsibility for their own professional development. They figure out what they need to learn and then collaborate with others to construct the knowledge they need. Instead of waiting for professional learning to be organized and delivered to them, connected learners contribute, interact, share ideas, and reflect.

Expert learners seek patterns in information, use "conditionalized" knowledge (Bransford, Brown, & Cocking, 1999, p. 43), and retrieve aspects of knowledge more easily. Viewing learning through the lens of an expert learner helps us inform our own learning and approach to new concepts. In addition, understanding how people learn in a connected world is essential when designing student learning experiences.

Learning in the Classroom

Understanding how we learn can affect how we design learning experiences for others. Many teach in the same way they were taught or lead the same way they were led. Sheryl homeschooled her children when they were young and led her local homeschool organization. Each year, she noticed that those new to home-schooling set up replicas of the classrooms they had experienced. They bought textbooks and a globe and arranged seats in rows facing the front of the room. They designed instruction by dividing disciplines into time segments. All they lacked were timed bells and fire drills. Sheryl was amazed that, given the opportunity to redesign education to meet personal needs, nine out of ten beginners reverted to the familiar.

That model—desks in rows, a teacher telling, and an administrator dictating and delegating—is found everywhere. But it is outdated and disconnected from the reality of a globally connected population, designed to produce obedient, rule-following factory workers and taxpayers. In his book *Linchpin* (2010), Seth Godin shares Woodrow Wilson's thoughts on public education:

> We want one class of persons to have a liberal education, and we want another class of persons, a very much larger class, of necessity, in every society, to forgo the privileges of a liberal education and fit themselves to perform specific difficult manual tasks. (p. 46)

Traditional schools were designed to create dutiful citizens who earned a living, paid their taxes on time, and kept things going in a capitalist democracy. The idea was to get uneducated newcomers to America off the streets and help them gain the knowledge and skills to secure factory jobs. Interestingly, that educational design improved the quality of life for many of the children for whom a free education was a step up. The common thought was that affluent parents would make sure their children received what they needed to live interesting lives (Godin, 2010).

Producing a skilled workforce in the past required standardization that was easily replicable across classrooms—a need for a predictable curriculum and methods. Drill and practice may have prepared a generation of factory workers, but it will not educate learners for tomorrow's world of work. Schools have habitually prepared students for life by making them dependent on others to teach them, rather than placing power over learning into the learner's hands. Classrooms that operate like connected learning communities—where students do meaningful work related to service learning and social justice—prepare students for *their* futures, not ours.

Putting It in Practice—In the Classroom

Shelley Wright, a high school educator from Moose Jaw, Saskatchewan, Canada, is a connected learner. Through blogging at http://shelleywright .wordpress.com, Shelley opens a transparent window onto her practice. She tweets (@wrightsroom), and she "truly believe[s] in the power of inquiry, collaborative, and project-based learning" as a means of do-it-yourself learning for both herself and her students.

In 2010 to 2011, her classroom changed radically. Her syllabus was on a wiki, and her content increased in rigor and was aligned more closely with the National Council of Teachers of English 21st Century Literacies. The sound and look of her classroom changed, too. Instead of students taking notes while she lectured on concepts from the novels they read about the Holocaust, groups of students researched ideas and created visual timelines on Dipity (www.dipity .com), which were then embedded on the student wiki.

The students' final projects encompassed all the standards and objectives Shelley had taught. The difference was that the process wasn't *taught*, it was student initiated, student designed, and student created. Learning culminated with a Holocaust Museum that students created. The most striking display may have been an illustration of the three-hundred-calorie-a-day food intake of those in the concentration camps (see http:// animoto.com/play/0aZonPHuwD4I6q83HXGE4w?utm_content=escape _link). Shelley's role in her classroom shifted dramatically. "My favourite part of student-centred [*sic*] learning is that I don't sit there and watch, or walk around listening to their conversations and making sure they're on task," she says. "I'm part of it. I help create, research, and problem-solve. I'm a co-learner" (Wright, 2011a).

Students' roles also shifted. Shelley notes, "I think [students] should be in control of what the project looks like and determining its outcome, but that, too, is a scenario they are not familiar with. My students are not used to determining their own learning. They're used to being told what to do" (Wright, 2011c).

Shelley has had to find ways to facilitate students learning such skills as synthesis and using information to create something new. While the change can be a struggle, she says the results are worth the effort. "Tomorrow we'll continue to press forward," she notes. "At times the learning curve is incredibly steep. But sometimes you need to step into the confusion for real learning to occur" (Wright, 2011c).

In addition to shifts in content and pedagogy, Shelley has adjusted assessment. Students choose three-fourths of their assignments for her to assess. Shelley relates:

I've chosen to do it this way so that my students feel the freedom to play and to fail. Perfectionists have a hard time playing when they fear their mark hangs in the balance. And many of my students

continued →

> *are intimidated by technology. So this allows the best of both worlds.*
> *It allows them the freedom to take chances and to have a voice in*
> *their assessment. (Wright, 2011b)*
>
> What if learning in your classroom were more like this? What if the goal of education were to help our students self-organize around learning objectives? What if we intentionally sought to produce connected, global, do-it-yourself learners in our students? Imagine the possibilities. Our classrooms would be transformed into places where we inspire students' creativity and help them see themselves as leaders and active contributors to knowledge building.

Where Are We?

Connected learning for connected teaching is self-directed and inquiry-based. It begins with your inquiry into a topic of interest, with your thirst to answer a question. You seek resources from your personal learning network, perhaps using your blog or Twitter. You deepen your understanding of new concepts. You evaluate their appropriateness, and you incorporate what you've learned into your practice. You return to your connected community to continuously and transparently share what you are learning. You are on your way to becoming a connected learner rather than simply being a networked teacher.

Where to Now?

Connected learning is collaborative learning that flourishes and thrives in a collaborative culture. That culture develops deep and meaningful human relationships with colleagues that enable us to have messy conversations that we use to create a better learning experience for students. With that common purpose, we invite you to look at the place of relationships, trust, collegiality, a shared vision, and deepened understanding of the stages of collaboration in creating connected learning. In chapter 4, we discuss the essential ingredients for building a collaborative culture that can dramatically alter not only our practice but also children's learning.

Get Connected

In the film *Star Wars: The Empire Strikes Back*, Yoda admonishes Luke Skywalker, "You must unlearn what you have learned." Unlearning and relearning doesn't apply only to levitating Luke's X-wing out of the bog. You re-envision yourselves as connected learners, unlearning all of those elements we discussed previously. We want to hear on Wallwisher what you will unlearn and relearn. Wallwisher is a collaborative virtual noticeboard that lets users post virtual sticky notes, including images, notes, video, and links. Visit http://wallwisher.com/demo to view a demo wall.

1. Go to http://wallwisher.com, and create an account.

2. Visit http://wallwisher.com/wall/unlearn.

3. Create a sticky note that answers these questions:

   - What do you have to unlearn and relearn about education, teaching, the classroom, or learning?

   - What are some challenges along the way?

Chapter Four

Building a Collaborative Culture

The nature of relationships among the adults within a school has a greater influence on the character and quality of that school and on student accomplishment than anything else.

—Roland Barth, author, consultant, and former faculty member, Harvard Graduate School of Education

Our Stories

Conversations within an online community of practice have led to deep, connected learning among educators throughout Ohio, Texas, and Louisiana. Consider this snapshot:

Karen: I am the director of curriculum and instruction. I believe that all children can learn and we need to get it right for them. My husband and I began building our log home 10 years ago and are still working on finishing this project. Maybe we should put the project on YouTube:)

Lani: Welcome!!! What a wonderful project!!! Hope that you'll share what has been most challenging and rewarding to this point. Do you have photos or video of all that has happened along the way?

Karen: I will share some photos and video. Unfortunately, the only video is when we took a direct hit from lightning four years ago and a third of it burned down. I guess the good part was that when we rebuilt that third, it was better.

Susan: Glad to meet another director of curriculum and instruction. What does that mean in your neck of the woods? P.S. Hello from Houston.

Donna: What is it like to build a log cabin? My husband is HUGE into house projects. I can't imagine building an entire house!!!

By including ways to get to know one another as well as sharing our learning, our collaborative wayfinding leads us to a deeper understanding of how technology can support authentic, inquiry-based learning.

—Lani

Educators make education meaningful and relevant for themselves and their students by co-creating learning and sharing. By collaborating, connected educators shift the existing school culture and self-actualize at the same time.

Collaboration is sometimes a difficult concept in traditional environments. As one group straightforwardly notes, "The culture of teachers sharing pedagogical strategies is not well established" (Barab, Moore, Cunningham, & ILF Design Team, 2000, p. 2). The lack of collaboration exists despite the finding that "change is more likely to be effective and long lasting if the teachers are allowed to build vital relationships with each other" (Barab, MaKinster, & Moore, 2001, p. 72).

In creating connected learning, the focus is on culture and the importance of shared ideals (Bezzina & Vidoni, 2006). Culture, an organization's or a group's way of doing things, is based on values, norms, and beliefs. Changing elements of culture is sometimes called re-culturing.

Changing values, norms, and beliefs may be necessary in order to support connected learning. Shared vision, shared values, a belief in learning for all, a collaborative environment, opportunities for inquiry, reflection, and "norms of continuous learning and improvement" (Peterson, 2002) encourage a culture of collaboration. In a culture of collaboration, learning thrives.

Re-culturing becomes possible when all stakeholders are involved in studying how to change the culture. Encouraging creativity and imagination (Manz, 1998) contribute to what Bezzina and Vidoni (2006) call an inner edge:

> This inner edge comes from relating differently with ourselves and one another. It requires a deeper knowledge about self and a deeper connection with our purpose for living. It means being mission-driven rather than having a mission. It means working as vigorously inside ourselves as we do on the outside, material world of schooling. It means acknowledging that the unseen spirit that builds bridges with the self and with others cannot be ignored. (p. 42)

Most professional development opportunities fail to encourage the collaborative construction of knowledge of practice. The lack of an intentional culture that supports sharing undermines educators' ability to collaborate. How do we build a collaborative culture that could serve as the catalyst for transforming education? What must be in place for connected educators to realize their greatest potential? With access to free technologies that readily support relationship building, collaboration could not be easier. Collaboration grows from relationships in which trust, collegiality, shared vision, and group development flourish.

Put Relationships First

Relationships matter. A lot. Relationships matter so much that we intentionally positioned this discussion immediately after making a case for becoming a learner. We feel the two are connected.

In your face-to-face social interactions through a serendipitous or intentional encounter, you often begin with a greeting and some brief personal information. The same is true with social, connected learning. The simple "Good morning, how was your drive in?" at school or the 140-character "Morning all. A smoky, cool, supposed-to-be-rainy-soon day ahead" on Twitter are invitations to conversations that can be the building blocks of relationships. These interactions become the bases for getting to know each other and finding common perspectives and experiences.

Fostering, nurturing, and maintaining positive, congenial relationships is the first step toward building collaborative cultures—in your school and in a more global connected learning community. This is a step away from the adversarial relationships in schools that prevent us from collectively working for the best interests of children (Barth, 2006).

Schools need both congenial and collegial relationships. Roland Barth (2006) suggests that congenial relationships, those that are personal and positive and thrive in most schools, are a condition for developing collegial relationships in which conversations center on practice.

There is a subtle but important difference between congeniality and collegiality. *Congeniality* refers to the polite, friendly relationship we have with one another, and it parallels nicely with our earlier discussion about cooperation. We see congeniality when we are sharing resources, talking about the latest episode of our favorite television show, complimenting a new bulletin board, or attending each other's birthday or retirement celebrations.

Collegiality is something more. *Collegiality* is a shared belief that none of us is as good (or smart) as all of us, and we can all contribute to improved individual practice. In connected communities, colleagues move beyond being polite and sociable to a place of hard work and risk for everyone involved. Cooperation and congeniality keep things pleasant. Collaboration and collegiality may produce some stormy weather, but they make things happen. They move teacher development beyond individual reflection, or reliance on external experts, to a point where we can learn from one another, sharing and building expertise together. Collegiality can be elusive and be difficult to establish. A great question to ask yourself is, "Is my group congenial or collegial?"

The secret to creating deep and trusting relationships is providing opportunities to share. When we participate, we connect, and from those connections come opportunities to collaborate around shared passions. Relationships that mature over time through everyday sharing and participation establish trust. When teachers establish trust through conversations about daily activities such as classroom practice, experience has shown that improved pedagogy and student success result.

Think About

Do collegial relationships abound in your network and local and global communities? Can you think of specific examples? If not, what can you do to encourage and nurture them? How can you celebrate others' success in your learning communities?

Establishing Trust

Trust, according to Megan Tschannen-Moran (2011), is one party's willingness to be vulnerable to another based on the confidence that the other is benevolent, reliable, competent, honest, and open. Trust, empathy, and reciprocity bond members together in any community or social setting, but even more so online (Preece, 2004). These elements are precursors to the knowledge sharing that helps us solve problems and achieve shared goals. As Nichani and Hung (2002) note:

> Trust is the glue that binds the members of a community to act in a sharing and adapting manner. Without trust, members would hoard their knowledge and experience and would not go through the trouble of sharing with or learning from others. (p. 51)

What encourages trust? Do you trust someone when you believe that person will behave reasonably and will do what he or she says? Do feelings of empathy and reciprocity build trust for you? Do you find that the more you empathize, the more you feel that the other person is like you? Trust is formed when people do what they say they will do. It is no different in connected online communities.

Sheryl has built a collaborative culture over time by cultivating relationships on Twitter with people she trusts. She trusts people there to give honest, respectful feedback to her questions, and they trust her. But how did trust grow in an environment absent of body language, voice intonation, or eye contact? What will trust gain you in a connected space? She wondered if her network trusted her, and if so, what did that mean? To find the answers, Sheryl tweeted:

> I am thinking about trust. Trust in connected, collaborative cultures. Do you guys trust me? Why or why not? What should I consider?

The ensuing comments offered insights on how online trust develops. One networker shared, "I do trust you; a lot rides on reputation and our interactions.

You treat me with respect. That helps in the trust area." Another: "Yes, I trust you. Initially, it came from perceived similarities, then was reinforced by how you treated people and their ideas." A Canadian teacher shared, "I trust you, I think originally because your reputation as an educator preceded you." So trust is reciprocal in some ways; Sheryl was trusted because she trusted others in the network, and their trust spread.

Reputation management is another important trust-building tool in online spaces. As one networker said, "The footprint helps. Just like we tell our kids, it tells a story. It is a tattoo of who you are." Building trust in an online environment, then, also means sharing enough of your real life work online to build credibility. "I think when online friends meet, they first check if f2f [face-to-face] and online realities match. If so, trust level remains the same."

Actions Online Matter

Others believed that online actions deeply influence trust levels. A New England teacher shared, "Trust is the result of a combination of shared values and repeated desired behaviors. For me, kindness, honesty, thoughtfulness. I think initial trust varies by person, too. Some assume the worst, some the best, most in between. Me—'innocent until proven guilty.'" Another educator agreed: "In my experience, trust takes a long time to build; it relies on someone doing the right thing many times over." Yet another added, "Trust depends on what the person says he/she will do, and then them doing it. It is more related to actions than time."

Transparency Is Important

The willingness to be a transparent learner (discussed in chapter 3) is also a trust-building factor. As one Twitter member said, "In a certain sense, I base trust online on how much the other person shares. Reciprocal. But also some info that gets shared with everyone." Another reiterated that view: "I tend to trust a person's online credibility by the caliber of work I see. I ask myself, does this person have a similar or higher transparency threshold?"

Other members of Sheryl's personal learning network also weighed in on transparency. An educator in the Netherlands said transparency is the catalyst for connected learning, that "being transparent makes what you share something from which all can learn." An administrator in a virtual school asked, "How do you truly connect without being transparent? It's so important in order to build trust." An elementary educator in an independent school in Virginia feels that transparency is essential; otherwise, she said, you are "simply *taking* from your personal learning network without giving back. Also, transparency enables you to get feedback from critical friends."

For the collective practice to evolve and subsequent collective efficacy to bud and bloom, connected co-learning must be transparent. It has been our experience that learning in the open is difficult for many educators. They believe they have nothing to say; they believe they are behind other learners and so remain quiet, fearing to put their thoughts out there.

Every individual, however, has a distinct perspective. You have learned something that could be just the piece others need to make sense of their own learning. Sharing those insights is critical to others and can be accomplished in ways that only networked learning can provide. As Siemens (2009) states, "It is when we make our learning transparent, we become teachers."

Creating Trust

Sobero (2008) suggests trust is created by:

- Developing relationships
- Identifying with the mission of the community and with the other members
- Generating feelings of belonging and mutual respect
- Openly sharing learning while building on knowledge about the practice, co-contributing to build content
- Developing community norms that encourage truthfulness, openness, routine collaboration, and the ability to address difficult issues or conflict

---

When connected learners work together to co-create content online, a basis for trust begins to develop. For example, in an online trust-building exercise Lani leads, she asked members to share a photo taken from the window of their workplace or a photo that created a digital story about some aspect of their lives. One member who posted a photo from her home office noted that, despite the oncoming winter, her hydrangeas were still blooming. A colleague from a southern state shared how his had died in a severe drought and how much he missed the Midwest, his former home. Another posted a picture of her family room after a child's birthday party and noted how all the trappings were less important than the memories she was creating by spending time with her children. In response, a co-learner replied how much he could empathize both with the state of the family room and her feelings about her children. The interactions in the process of co-creating content encouraged trust among these learners.

Connected learners have to work harder to establish trust. In face-to-face interactions, we get to know people over time through causal interactions. We see them come in, take off their coats, and complain about traffic. We get to know their families through pictures on their desks and through conversations about a baby's fever and children's sports. The steps are the same, but shared in business-as-usual ways. We do not have to create intentional acts to share this information. In online spaces, we can have many of the same casual interactions if we think through how to make them happen. Intentional acts have the same trust-building effect as those that occur naturally. We upload pictures, type stories about our children, create and share videos of sports events, and tweet about traffic jams.

Through those interactions:

> Community members often develop a shared way of doing things, a set of common practices, and a greater sense of common purpose. Sometimes they formalize these in guidelines and standards, but often they simply remain "what everybody knows" about good practice. In the course of helping each other, sharing ideas, and collectively solving problems, "everybody" often becomes a trusted group of peers. (McDermott, 2001)

Within connected learning communities, norms of etiquette can help provide boundaries within which acceptable behavior occurs and allows trust to develop. Communities in the initial stages need to explore norms of etiquette. As the community matures, standards of etiquette become embedded in the community's character (Preece, 2004). For trust to develop naturally, standards should be clear, not imposed, codeveloped, and consistent.

Think About

How do we build a collaborative culture in online spaces? What are the needed components? What does it look like? What should the connected learner do to make collaboration happen?

Fostering Collegiality

Because collegiality is difficult to achieve, we should consider how genuine collegial relationships are formed. Collegial relationships create real change. Collegial relationships are characterized by conversations about practice, problems, and solutions to learning challenges for all students, and about ways to improve the school overall. In collegial relationships, connected educators share ideas and challenge each other's thinking. They observe each other's work face to face or through video, and they reflect, with a respectful but critical eye, on practice. Listening, understanding, and empathizing also are marks of collegial relationships (Peterson, 1994).

When we refer to *collegiality,* we refer to that which is genuine. In many schools, collegiality is contrived and structured. Hargreaves (1994) makes an important distinction between *genuine* collaboration and collegiality and *contrived* collaboration and collegiality. Genuine collaboration and collegiality are distinguished by spontaneity and by being voluntary; the acts are unpredictable and development oriented. Contrived collegiality is noted for being administratively regulated, compulsory, scheduled, and predictable. According to Hargreaves (1994), mandated or contrived collegiality

> makes it difficult for programs to be adjusted to the purposes and practicalities of particular school and classroom settings. It overrides teacher professionalism and the discretionary judgment which comprises it. And it diverts teachers' efforts and energies into simulated compliance with administrative demands that are inflexible and inappropriate for the settings in which they work. (p. 208)

To foster collegiality, local, face-to-face professional learning communities use organizational norms that nurture and support collegial dialogue. They exchange ideas, debate issues, and cooperate rather than compete. Collegiality is fostered in face-to-face settings when grade-level teams, interdisciplinary units, or departments make time to meet, talk, think, and interact using teacher-led protocols to discuss shared practice. When time, depth, and sincerity are not present and the dialogue lacks richness, the results are often complaints, whining, and excuses. Administrators encourage teacher leaders and nurture collegiality by providing them time and a place to collaborate (Peterson, 1994). Equally important, practitioners in collegial relationships root for one another (Barth, 2006). Celebration of and for each other is an important component in connected learning communities. Community leaders, both in online and offline spaces, need to develop protocols for identifying and sharing good news.

In our work through Powerful Learning Practice, sharing craft knowledge and celebrating work are commonplace. For example, in the Powerful Learning Practice blog (http://plpnetwork.com/blog), community leaders regularly share with global readers the exciting news and accomplishments of participants (called PLPeeps). In addition, the Powerful Learning Practice newsletter *Top Shelf* has a regular section called "Meet the Peep," which features a community member. Powerful Learning Practice community members regularly share craft knowledge developed in groups where fellow PLPeeps serve as a critical friends. Members also are invited to contribute to the blog Voices from the Learning Revolution (http://plpnetwork.com/voices) as a way to build capacity and celebrate their ideas and work in their schools.

These collegial relationships set the stage for us to become better educators.

Putting It in Practice—In the School

Faced with the common problem, a professional learning community at the Chinquapin School in Highlands, Texas, decided to view senioritis as a symptom of a larger problem—student and faculty burnout caused by traditional teaching where creativity and innovation are stifled (http://chinquapinlearningedge.wikispaces.com/Home).

Teachers questioned how to break the cycle. Their involvement in a community of practice led them to develop the model for using a culminating senior project intended to engage students in authentic learning, return joy to learning, and immerse students in developing skills for the 21st century. This shift in learning and teaching would, in essence, change the very culture of their school (http://chinquapin.wikispaces.com/Culminating+Senior+Project).

In the summer prior to and during the pilot experience, incoming seniors and faculty read Daniel Pink's book *Drive* (Pink, 2009). The seniors and the school's dean, Susan, shared their thoughts on a group blog, The Learning Edge (http://chinquapinlearningedge.blogspot.com). Faculty professional learning was ongoing throughout the year. As the project scales up over time,

> *an eighth-grade project will be a primary entrance criterion for admission to the high school. During high school, students will refine their final project topics and undertake research, employ resources outside the school . . . , use web 2.0 tools to share their work in a transparent way, and build toward a final project that will set them apart—our students will become leaders on the learning edge. (Chinquapin Learning Edge, n.d.)*

Creating a Shared Vision

In a shared vision that articulates our aspirations for the future of learning, we find not only hope to move forward, but also momentum to go beyond hope to the work that will move us toward the transformation we wish to see. Senge (1990a) notes, "The practice of shared vision involves the skills of unearthing shared 'pictures of the future' that foster genuine commitment and enrollment rather than compliance" (p. 9). In the process of developing a shared vision for the future of learning, educators share concerns about the current reality and then talk about their deepest hopes and dreams for the future. From answers to questions such as, What do you see right now? and What would like to see in the future? come a creative tension that leads to collaboration. Shared vision becomes about "creating something new together" (Senge, 2000, p. 302). Visions, like other aspects of education, should not be *done to us* but created collectively and revisited regularly.

Leadership's Role

By defining leadership as constructivist learning, Linda Lambert (1998) emphasizes:

> The key notion in this definition is that leadership is about learning together, and constructing meaning and knowledge collectively and collaboratively. It involves opportunities to surface and mediate perceptions, values, beliefs,

> information, and assumptions through continuing conversa-
> tions; to inquire about and generate ideas together; to seek,
> to reflect upon and make sense of work in the light of shared
> beliefs and new information; and to create actions that grow
> out of these new understandings. Such is the core of leader-
> ship. (pp. 5–6)

A shared vision that connects to passion, day-to-day work, and school improvement is important in creating a collaborative culture that supports the connected
learner. Leaders can create this kind of vision statement either by themselves or
collaboratively. The advantages of involving others in creating a vision are a greater
degree of commitment, engagement, and diversity of thought, all attributes of
healthy learning organizations.

A first step toward shared vision making is to ask stakeholders questions such as:

- "What are our guiding principles for how we should operate and work
  together?"

- "Why do we exist?"

- "What do we want to create?"

- "What should school look like to support the needs of today's learners?"

Using established conversation protocols is another way to develop a shared
vision. For example, Café Conversations (www.theworldcafe.com), Everyday
Democracy (www.everyday-democracy.org), National School Reform Faculty
(www.nsrfharmony.org/protocol/protocols.html), and Future Search (www.future
search.net) all have techniques that can work in online spaces or face-to-face to
achieve shared goals and fast action.

Understanding the Stages of Collaboration

You've formed your group, whether a grade-level team at your school or a group
in an online community, and you're ready to collaborate and change the world. You
have your first get-together, then your second, and you leave bitterly disappointed.
The deep and meaningful collaboration you had imagined has not occurred. Your
colleagues likely share your feelings. Be not discouraged or dismayed; various
models have been proposed to explain how groups move through developmental
stages. Tuckman's (1965) model helps outline what to expect as your group comes
together.

Forming

Tuckman says groups first go through the process of forming when team members get to know one another. Members are often excited as they anticipate starting something new. Congeniality is evident in their interactions. This stage also

is often characterized by member reluctance toward openness, as trust has not been established yet.

Storming

Once the group is formed and members move past the excitement of trying something new, the novelty wears off. People begin to disagree and become frustrated by the time it takes to learn something new or by the inconvenience and inefficiency of not being just told what to do. Self-directed learning and collective construction of knowledge is hard work. Disagreements and conflicts arise around how to proceed. One member takes the lead and may be challenged. Some groups may forge ahead and attempt to ignore underlying currents of dissatisfaction.

We have found that if educators are not told that storming is a normal part of the connected learning community growth process, they give up prematurely, assuming this is one more professional development strategy that does not work.

Norming

Often teams get to a point that they know a deadline is coming and decide to forge ahead. As the term implies, the group members develop norms or accepted behaviors for how they will operate as a group. Teams at this stage push through the dissonance, realizing that since they are expected to learn as a team, they might as well figure out how to get the work done.

Performing

With norms and relationships established, the group enters the performing stage, when teams move past congeniality to collegiality. Conversations focus on achieving the group's goals. Messy conversations, inquiry, and deep learning become the norm. A culture of collaboration has been established.

Although the stages are often described in a linear manner, groups can move among any of the stages other than forming at different times in their collaboration (Atherton, 2011). It is also important to note that teams can get stuck at a stage and might need outside intervention from someone serving as a critical friend. Your and your colleagues' awareness of this model can inform and facilitate your work as you collaborate.

Put People's Needs at the Forefront

Any significant educational transformation creates people issues. Teachers will be asked to challenge the status quo, engage in mutual accountability, change to match job descriptions, and develop new skills. In general, school staff will be unsettled and resist these changes. A grieving process often occurs as educators adapt to the loss of ideas and strategies in which they have invested so much.

Most people think of grieving in connection with the death of a loved one. But we grieve for many reasons—the loss of a job, the end of a relationship, or anything that causes significant change in our lives.

Grieving can trigger a host of unfamiliar and confusing emotions and behaviors. In learning communities, this change can be managed with a shared approach through learning communities focusing on the human aspects of the shift. Working in teams ensures that individual issues are addressed rather than ignored, often without putting at risk the speed of adoption, morale, or achievement. Make time for members of your learning community to talk through and adjust to change initiatives and the transformation taking place in order to build a community that will last and be effective.

Think About

Have you given yourself time to grieve the loss of *business as usual* in your journey toward becoming a connected learner? How could you provide this opportunity for others in your school or connected learning community who are also feeling the loss of all things familiar?

Model Collaboration in Practice

Technology has thinned classroom and school walls, blurred the boundaries of time and space, and has provided opportunities for authentic teacher learning in networks and communities. Through technology, we gain a deeper understanding of the world and help prepare students for an unknown future. Authentic learning, according to Zhao (2009), requires:

> a global perspective, a deep understanding of the interconnectedness and interdependence of all human beings; a set of global skills—cultural knowledge and linguistic abilities that enable them to appreciate and respect other cultures and peoples and interact with other people; and global attitudes—emotional and psychological capacities to manage the anxiety and complexity of life in a globalized world. (p. 192)

To thrive in the increasingly globalized world, we need to help students feel comfortable collaborating with people from different cultures and negotiating cultural differences in both physical and virtual worlds. Before we can model these skills for our students, we must own them ourselves.

Putting It in Practice—In the Classroom

In Ann Michaelsen's classroom at Sandvika High School, on the outskirts of Oslo, Norway, her English as a second language students recently videotaped an in-person interview with Moliehi Sekese, a teacher from the tiny African nation of Lesotho. Sekese, who teaches in a remote school with no direct access to the Internet, was in Norway at Ann's invitation, after first meeting her at an international Microsoft Innovative Education conference and becoming part of her personal learning network.

In a blog post for Powerful Learning Practice's "Voices from the Learning Revolution," Ann (Michaelsen, 2011) writes:

> *Keeping in touch is not easy when the only Internet option you have in Lesotho is a distant Internet café. Moliehi has an amazing story to tell—about how one teacher with determination and an innovative mind could win a technology competition representing a school with eight hundred students, two computers, and no electricity.*

Drawing on other personal learning network connections, Ann was able to raise funds for Sekese to visit schools in both Norway and Sweden and spend time with students exchanging stories about their very different cultures and what it's like to be a teenager in their respective nations.

> *Moliehi has a wonderful ability to reach out to teachers and young people alike, with a clear message. As one student wrote: "Listening to her presentation made us realize how lucky we are here in Norway. We have food, clean drinking water, clothes, textbooks, and computers."*

Because Ann's students all blog (and some have earned a global audience), they were able to share what they learned. They've kept in touch with Sekese through her comments on their blogs, and she has shared the Norway teenagers' writings with her own students in Lesotho. "With the use of technology like this blogging," Sekese wrote on one student blog, "it shows clearly that the world can become one village where everyone is learning from one another. . . . I hope one day we will be able to collaborate on different issues [from school to school]."

Here's what Ann draws from the experience:

> *This encounter would not have been possible without my ability to connect through Facebook, Twitter, Skype, and blogs. All these social media tools combined give you the power to create learning networks on a global scale. And the benefits are not yours alone. Your students will soon learn to appreciate how open the world has become! (Michaelsen, 2011)*

Where Are We?

- Fostering, nurturing, and maintaining positive relationships is the first step toward building collaborative cultures.

- Trust is an absolute necessity and a precursor to the knowledge sharing needed to solve problems and achieve shared goals.

- Actions online do matter, and transparency affects trust in online relationships.

- Building trust takes contact, communication, time, and certification from others.

- Collegiality in collaborative relationships is valuable.

- Shared vision, like other aspects of education, should not be done to us but collectively created and regularly revisited.

- Group development typically takes place in several stages.

- Global collaboration is an important skill for living and thriving in the increasingly globalized world.

Think About

What are the first steps you will take in organizing a connected learning community for your school? How will you communicate a need for and garner buy-in toward a collaborative culture?

Where to Now?

Now that we understand connected learning, have taken a learner's posture, and have the basics for collaboration, we will explore specific tools before learning how to create a personal learning network. In chapter 5, we turn to tools and emerging web technologies that support collaboration and collective learning, in particular for documenting and archiving learning, for connecting and collaborating, and for extending student learning.

Get Connected

A shared vision emerges from the intersection of professional learning community members' personal visions. First, however, connected learners must develop personal visions through their personal learning network. In this activity, we collaborate on Google Docs to create a shared vision. (See the tutorial at http://docs.google.com/demo/edit?id=scADZumY05l0xmrm-N0UT7GN3 &dt=spreadsheet#document, if you are not familiar with Google Docs.)

You'll need a Google account to use Google Docs. Many connected learners use Google Docs to collaborate and to keep notes.

1. Go to www.google.com/accounts/NewAccount to sign up for an account.

2. Fill out the form and click on *I accept. Create my account.*

3. Keep your username (probably your personal email address) and password in a secure place that you can access in case you forget them.

4. One tip is to use the same login name across Web 2.0 tools so others can find you.

The next step is where the connecting begins.

1. Go to www.google.com/docs, and login with your Google account.

2. Visit http://bit.ly/hxsC5y for our shared vision Google Doc slideshow.

3. Create your own slide within our slideshow that answers the following questions. The *we* refers to all connected learners, networked teachers, and educators reading this book.

    *   What are our guiding principles for how we should operate and work together?

    *   Why do we exist?

    *   What do we want to create?

    *   What should school look like to support the needs of today's learners?

When you create your slide, add images and be sure to use a template that expresses how you feel and shows your personality.

Chapter Five

Using Tools to Support Connected Learning

Technology as an enabler of learning . . . and of creating connections. The Internet has revealed that large fields of knowledge are given value when connected. Technology in communities is essentially just a means of creating fluidity between knowledge segments . . . and connecting people.

—George Siemens, researcher on learning, The University of Athabasca

Our Stories

Tools have always been an important part of my life as an educator. I am a project-, problem-, passion-based teacher who believes students need both hands-on and visceral learning. I believe knowledge construction comes from experiencing or building something yourself or collectively as a team using tools. The more powerful the tools, the better, whether power tools used to construct a Swiss Family Robinson–type tree house or Web 2.0 tools used to create a Think Quest (www.thinkquest.org) competition piece. However, I feel it is a disservice to children when educators become so enthralled with the tools that they lose sight of what is most important—the learning. Our focus should always be on what we can do with the tool. Tools should be used to serve the learning. Blink, and online tools change, so be careful where you invest your time.

—Sheryl

We have explored the important concepts underlying connected learning, including seeing ourselves as learners first and learning the fundamentals of collaboration. As we explore technological tools that enable connected learning to occur, keep in mind that tools are not helpful unless users understand the context in which tools can best improve learning. We will review tools for documenting and archiving learning, tools for connecting and collaborating, and tools for extending student learning.

You do not need to be a web expert to take advantage of these tools—many of them are used widely because they are easy to use. The best way to understand the tools is to experiment with them. You may want to tinker as you read to get a basic understanding, or you may note those that might be helpful in your own context and explore them more deeply later when we discuss creating a personal learning network.

We lay out what you need to understand to use each tool and then offer examples of how to put the tool into practice. The explanations are most helpful to novice social media users. If you are well versed in Web 2.0, you may want to scan this chapter for highlights about how a tool can be used in various contexts. Whether you're a beginner or an expert, consider searching YouTube (www.youtube.com) for more advanced tutorials showcasing additional features and benefits of each of the tools explained in this chapter. Visit **go.solution-tree.com/technology** for live links to these tools.

Tip

The first step in using each tool is to set up an account with a username and password for the website. We highly recommend using the same username and password for each site in your learning network, as it is easier to remember this way.

Tools for Documenting and Archiving Learning

There are lots of tools online for keeping track of what you've found on the web. Here are a few that we think will be most valuable for you and your classroom.

Social Bookmarking

By some estimates, the World Wide Web has more than fifteen billion webpages and it is growing exponentially (de Kunder, n.d.). To avoid information overload and be more efficient, you need to categorize and archive the content you want. Social bookmarking is a useful and fun way to organize it while connecting with friends and colleagues and discovering new articles and links along the way.

Just as a library uses categories and keywords as part of the Dewey Decimal System, the web uses categories and keywords, or tags, to arrange content for simple archiving and retrieval.

What Is Tagging?

Tagging, also known as *social bookmarking* or *folksonomy*, is a way to organize the content (such as websites, photos, videos, and blog posts) you access online by grouping similar items together under labels. These labels, called *tags*, are keywords that you use to describe the content you are organizing for easier retrieval later. Many blogs you read offer tags for posts that allow you to find all posts corresponding to those particular keywords or phrases. Other popular websites that rely on tagging include Delicious (www.delicious.com), Diigo (www.diigo.com), Flickr (www.flickr.com), and YouTube (www.youtube.com). In this book, we have used common tags to help you get more information about the topics being highlighted.

In the early days of the web (Web 1.0), you might have bookmarked useful websites using your web browser and archived the address to use later. You may have arranged your bookmarks in folders and named your folders, such as *teaching strategies* for teaching websites or *research* for articles you found online.

In Web 2.0, archiving is a collaborative effort (hence the term *social* in *social media*). Not only can you bookmark websites for personal use and assign multiple tags or keywords to help organize them, you can also share this information within a network of connected learners. In turn, you benefit from the bookmarks shared by those in your network.

Delicious

Delicious (www.delicious.com) is a popular website for bookmarking and tagging websites. Suppose you are seeking ideas for new strategies for your classroom, or perhaps your professional learning community or community of practice wants to compile resources on a topic, or perhaps you want to document and archive the links suggested in this book. You might start by googling. Each time you find an interesting webpage, include the web address in your Delicious account and add tags so you can find it again.

You may find it difficult to weed through thousands of Google search results. A more efficient way to find what you are looking for online is to tap into the collective knowledge of a social bookmarking (tagging) community. Using Delicious, you can search tags to find webpages other users have categorized that match your interest. Using this presort saves time. Remember to bookmark the pages using your profile and tag them for easy retrieval.

You also can connect with other educators who share your research interests. As you search on Delicious, you will notice that some people have a wealth of information for your particular tag or topic. You can add that user to your network, and even subscribe (see the section on RSS below) to that user's tag, helping you build a connected learning network.

Diigo

Diigo (www.diigo.com) is a social bookmarking community, similar to Delicious, but with enhanced features. By installing Diigo's browser add-on, you can make annotations right on the webpages you visit, highlighting information or adding sticky notes to the pages. The site is divided into three sections: My Library, My Network, and My Groups.

My Library is best for research. Here you can bookmark webpages, highlight a section of interest, add a sticky note to the site, and then save it to your library for easy retrieval. *My Network* allows you to build a personal learning network by following or connecting with people who share your research interests. Imagine that all of your colleagues were part of your Diigo network. Connecting on Diigo, you would have access not only to any interesting articles they bookmark online but any annotations (highlights or sticky notes) they added.

Diigo also takes social bookmarking a step further by allowing you to form collaborative groups. *My Groups* allows members of your local professional learning community or global community of practice to share documents as you explore, annotate, and make meaning by using the annotations and sticky notes. Designed with educators in mind, Diigo allows teachers to set up an account for each student in a class as well as to form a group for the class. Consider the possibilities for learning. You can create a group knowledge repository for each class; your students can add annotations and sticky notes as they read, helping each other as they collectively construct knowledge. Diigo also sends group members email alerts when new information is posted.

To access these premium features on Diigo, be sure to sign up as an educator. Diigo is also designed for educators to find and network with other educators to form a personal learning network. Search under Diigo Groups for a topic of interest. For example, the group Web 2.0 Tools for Teachers has nine hundred members who are posting content and collaborating to learn how to use the tools we discuss in this chapter. Librarians, administrators, and curriculum directors also can find groups on Diigo.

Tools for Connecting and Collaborating

There are many resources online for connecting and collaborating to build your personal learning network. Here are a few that we think will be most useful for you and your classroom.

Blogs

Short for *weblog*, *blogs* are websites that are continually updated with journal-like entries, or posts, usually arranged in chronological order with the most recent appearing first. Blogs are great sources of ideas, information, and experiences about learning, leading, and teaching. At the time of this writing, there are an estimated 146 million blogs, and each day about 40,000 new ones are created (The Nielsen Company, 2010).

Blogs are a participatory medium where users welcome feedback and discussion. Many blogs allow comments at the bottom of each post. The Important Comment feature offers opportunities to engage in conversations about the writer's ideas or experiences. In addition, buttons below the post often allow you to easily share the blog content with friends via email, Facebook, Twitter, and other media.

Blogs have become the fastest-growing personal publishing medium (The Nielsen Company, 2010) because blogging platforms such as Blogger (www .blogger.com), WordPress (http://wordpress.com), and Tumblr (http://tumblr.com) all are free for users, allowing you to create your own blogging website in a matter of minutes without any knowledge of web design or HTML. Additional platforms geared for educators and their students are Edublogs (http://edublogs.org) and, for younger students, Kidblog (http://kidblog.org). You can easily become a blogger if you are not already. Your ideas and experiences with learning, leading, and teaching may significantly contribute to a more accomplished global practice.

Edublog

Edublog (http://edublogs.org) allows educators to communicate with students and parents. When you set up a blog, consider your purpose and audience. What do you want to communicate? Who is your audience? You may be willing to chronicle your practice, making it transparent and allowing others a window to your district, your building, or your classroom so that all can learn from you. You may want to create a blog coauthored by those in your professional learning community to record your journey as you collaborate to improve student learning.

A blog can provide all stakeholders—students, teachers, parents, and the community—with current information on the school's events, issues, and celebrations, as well as provide a discussion forum. A classroom blog can facilitate local and global student collaboration and discussions, replacing a classroom newsletter or other printed or emailed forms and calendars. You can post regular updates about assignments and offer links to online course materials. This way, students and their parents can access all classroom information as well as interact with you in one place. Blogs can contain pictures, links, and videos, and your blog posts can be organized by categories and tags so that topics can be easily located. Your students can post or comment on the class blog and even create their own blogs. With an

Edublog, you may opt to keep your blog private, allowing only a specified group of people to participate, or you can open it to all audiences.

Setting up a blog is easy with the Edublog platform. The basic option for blogging is free, although you may be interested in paying for an upgraded account with more features. You do not need to know how to create a webpage. You can select from predesigned color themes and layouts, and then customize those themes for a unique design. You will find that creating and publishing a blog post is as simple as filling out an online form, much the way you enter a subject line and body text into a form to compose an email. Soon you and your students will be posting and collaborating while also keeping their parents informed of class activities.

RSS Readers

Blogs are not only about publishing, they're about reading, networking, and collaborating with other educators. Once you have discovered blogs you want to read regularly, you can subscribe to the blogs' RSS feeds using an RSS reader that brings new content to you rather than having to visit various websites to check them individually.

Imagine waking up each morning and scanning forty newspapers and twenty-five magazines for only the content that interests you in the time it takes to drink a cup of coffee. Impossible. However, you can easily scan hundreds of blogs within minutes, skimming through for just the information you need. While you can visit any blog by going directly to its web address, you can subscribe to blogs and be notified when the writer has a new post by using an RSS feed. Using an RSS reader, you can subscribe to many blogs and log onto one website to read all the new posts at one time, scanning posts by headlines or even by topic categories you have set up.

To find blogs to read, use a search engine, such as Google Blog Search (http://blogsearch.google.com), to search by keywords that interest you. Another option is to search using a blog directory, such as Support Blogging (http://supportblogging.com/Links+to+School+Bloggers), where you select educational blogs of teachers, administrators, librarians, researchers, and educational thought leaders.

To get started, explore each blog by reading the most recent post and by clicking on some links to view other pages on the blog. Bloggers love feedback. Leaving even a short comment tells the blogger that readers find the post informative and useful. If you find a blog post thought provoking or enjoyable, post a comment using the link at the bottom of the blog post. Comments help you connect with the blogger, whether for a friendly exchange or to ask a question.

Suggested Blogs

21st Century Collaborative: Sheryl Nussbaum-Beach, http://21stcenturycollaborative.com

The Fischbowl: Karl Fisch, http://thefischbowl.blogspot.com

Open Thinking: Alec Couros, http://educationaltechnology.ca/couros

Possibilities Abound: Lani Ritter Hall, http://possibilitiesabound.blogspot.com

Weblogg-ed: Will Richardson, http://weblogg-ed.com

These teacher leaders may challenge the way you see the world.

A Place at the Table: Susan Graham, http://blogs.edweek.org/teachers /place_at_the_table

Reflections of a Techie: Marsha Ratzel, http://teachingtechie.typepad.com

Teacher in a Strange Land: Nancy Flanagan, http://blogs.edweek.org /teachers/teacher_in_a_strange_land

TeachMoore: Renee Moore, http://teacherleaders.typepad.com/teachmoore

The Tempered Radical: Bill Ferriter, http://teacherleaders.typepad.com /the_tempered_radical

Educational blogs list: http://supportblogging.com/Links+to+School +Bloggers

Google Reader

Google Reader (http://reader.google.com) is a blog reader (also called a news aggregator) that will allow you to subscribe to the RSS feed of a blog you think is a good resource. To do this, sign up for a Google Reader or Bloglines (www .bloglines.com) account. The process for subscribing is similar to subscribing to an email newsletter that you then receive in your inbox each time it is published. Setting up a blog reader lets you read all of your blog feeds by logging in to one place. If you already have a Google account (for Gmail or iGoogle), you can use the same username and password to access Google Reader (as well as Google Docs, page 84).

You can subscribe to a blog in two ways. First, you can open Google Reader and click on Subscribe to a Blog on the top left of the webpage. You will be directed to search for a blog by keywords or to enter the blog's URL address—the directions you type in the address bar to tell the browser what page on the web you want to reach. Another method is to subscribe to the blog while you are on the blog's website. Most blogs provide a button to click if you would like to subscribe to the RSS feed. When you click on a Subscribe button from a blog's site, you will be asked what blog reader you use. You can then select, for example, Google if you are using Google Reader as your RSS reader.

Your Google Reader account might look similar to an email inbox. When a blog updates with a new post, you see the blog's headline bolded just like an unread email would look in your inbox. You click on the headline and the blog post will be displayed, just as clicking on an incoming email displays the message. The headline listings make scanning content very efficient. Before you know it, you will be scanning hundreds of blog posts at a time using Google Reader.

Podcasts

Learning comes through all forms of communication, not just the written word. Some of us learn better through audio formats rather than writing, and that's where podcasts come in. Listening to content or viewing videos should be part of your connected learning environment. Podcasts are audio or video files. Just as a television series has episodes, so do podcasts. Similar to subscribing to a blog and receiving an update each time a new post is published, you can subscribe to podcasts using RSS technology and be notified each time a new audio or video file is published. You can download a podcast on any number of topics. A host of people—large news organizations, Harvard professors, and even students—produce podcasts.

You can download podcasts to your computer and watch or listen from your desktop or laptop. You also can download a podcast to a portable media device, such as an iPod or other MP3 player, or a smartphone, such as an iPhone or BlackBerry. The benefit of podcasts is that you can download files and listen to them whenever you have time. Many people listen as they are commuting, traveling, taking a walk, or even cleaning the house. Creating and sharing your own podcast takes just a computer, the Internet, and a microphone. Students can be engaged and enjoy interactivity in the classroom by creating, producing, and sharing their own podcasts with others all over the world.

For example, the students at Willowdale Elementary School in Omaha, Nebraska, create podcast episodes to share about topics they are learning. For each episode, the students research a topic, such as the thirteen American colonies and aspects of life in colonial times or famous artists and their techniques, and then write scripts to share the information they learned with other students. The episodes feature theme music, and students take turns hosting.

Podomatic

Podomatic (www.podomatic.com) is a free tool to help you record, produce, and publish a web broadcast. Once you've created your account, you will see the My

Account button. From My Account, you will be able to create your first episode under the My Podcast tab. Click on Post New Episode. You will see an option to Record with Your Webcam or Microphone. If you are making an audio podcast, you need only a microphone; however, you can easily create a video podcast using your webcam. Make sure your microphone is plugged in and test it, then press Record and begin podcasting. When you are finished recording, preview the podcast and rerecord it if you are not happy with your first attempt. Once you are satisfied, opt to save the recording. You will be directed to input information about your episode, such as the title, description, and even a picture. Then click on Post Episode. Go back to your My Podcast page (it may take a minute to load), and you will be able to play your podcast. To share the podcast with listeners, provide them with the URL address for your My Podcast page.

Microblogs

Microblogging tools allow you to share information quickly and efficiently with your personal learning network.

Twitter

Twitter (www.twitter.com) is a microblogging service, accessed from your computer or mobile phone, which connects you to a worldwide network of people. Think of Twitter like a very short blog—Twitter's *tweets* are microposts of a maximum of 140 characters. Like blogs, the tweets may contain videos and photos, but these are shown as links in order to stay within the character limits. Just as you have readers and subscribers for your blog, you have *followers* on Twitter. Your followers see your messages (called tweets or updates) as you tweet them, along with the chronological tweets from all those they follow.

You will want to follow your own list of people in the Twitterverse. Your Twitter account homepage lists people you are following as well as your followers. The homepage also displays a chronological list of tweets from the people you are following. This list is called your Twitter stream, or timeline. You see it each time you log in to your Twitter account from its homepage (www.twitter.com).

When you set up your account, you select a username, often referred to as a *Twitter handle*. This name is how people will refer to you on Twitter. Adding the @ symbol to a username is the convention used for mentioning a person on Twitter. For example, if you wanted to refer to the president, your 140-character update would mention @WhiteHouse (the president's Twitter handle) or @pmharper for the prime minister of Canada. Twitter users often reply to each other, conversing by starting out a tweet with the person's Twitter handle. These conversations are public and may be read by anyone following those Twitter users.

You can send private messages to people on Twitter using the direct-messaging function. Direct messages work much the same way as email but, of course, are limited to 140 characters. Direct messaging can be useful for continuing a conversation privately that may have started in public tweets.

Another important component of Twitter is a hashtag. Like tags on a blog, hashtags are keywords that help organize the updates on Twitter. Hashtags begin with the # symbol and are searchable on Twitter. Try a Twitter search for these popular education hashtags: #edchat and #edreform. Anyone can create a hashtag simply by typing the # symbol followed by a keyword to make the tag searchable. In fact, we have created one for this book: #connectededc. Groups often form a Twitter chat around a hashtag, following updates using the hashtag. The hashtag provides a forum similar to a chat room, where everyone is invited to participate. To tweet as part of the chat, you simply include the hashtag at the end of your post. To view the chat, you perform a search (there is a search box on your profile home page) for all tweets containing the hashtag. Some educators have also begun to form hashtag groups and schedule weekly live conversations via Twitter, which are then archived on a wiki. Examples are #4thchat, #teachchat, #scichat, #engchat, and #ntchat (for new teachers). Visit http://bit.ly/twitter-chats for a growing list of such chat groups.

One benefit of Twitter is that because you are microblogging, your time investment is minimal. At the same time, the Twitterverse is large and diverse, and you can easily find a broad network of people with whom to connect and collaborate. Because of its mobile component, people often update and have conversations via Twitter on the fly using their mobile phones. These quick conversations offer an immediacy that is unmatched by other social networks. For example, the first photo of the 2009 US Airways Flight 1549 crash in the Hudson River was uploaded to Twitter by an eyewitness before news crews were on the scene (Beaumont, 2009).

The **Twitter website** is a good resource for connecting and collaborating with educators. When you first use Twitter, you will want to find people to follow. When you signed up for an account, Twitter probably suggested a list of well-known people to follow. You also will be able to search your email contacts for people you know who use Twitter. A great place to find people to follow on Twitter is on the Twitter4Teachers Wiki (http://twitter4teachers.pbworks.com). In addition, use Twitter Search (http://search.twitter.com) for keywords that interest you. For example, if you search for *teach* or *connected learning*, you may find other educators who are Twitter users. This will help you identify people on Twitter you may want to connect to and collaborate with. Once you've searched, you'll see the Follow button at the top of the page. Click on it to add that person to your feed.

If you see a Twitter update you would like to respond to, send that person a public reply by using the @username convention discussed earlier. The more you converse using Twitter, the more you will see in your Twitter stream that people are mentioning your username as well. You will quickly see how Twitter can become a resource for crowdsourcing information—outsourcing questions or tasks and asking for public input to develop the information. Once you have a large enough Twitter network following you, you will be able to tweet out questions (such as, "Do you use podcasts for teaching? I'm looking for examples.") and receive helpful answers instantly. You also will start receiving a lot of news and information on Twitter from the large network of people you follow.

While you can use the Twitter website to perform the necessary functions for connecting and collaborating, many users prefer **Twitter applications** that simplify the process. TweetDeck (www.tweetdeck.com) and HootSuite (www .hootsuite.com) are two applications available for your computer and smartphone. These applications act as a dashboard for all of your Twitter activity with a setup of vertical columns that you can customize. For example, you can access your Twitter stream in one column, view mentions of your tweets (your @mentions) in another, and view your direct messages in a third. You also can add customized columns. For example, you could create a column to conduct searches for keywords of interest.

Wikis

A wiki is a webpage that allows a group to work collaboratively by facilitating planning, collaboration, and project coordination. Wikis allow groups to compile documents and information all in one place. You can post links, videos, photos, and files to a wiki. Groups can edit the webpages together; anyone can change what appears on the wiki. Wikis also offer a separate section for threaded discussions.

Think about the last time you collaborated on a project. You may have emailed a document draft back and forth, each person taking turns making changes to it. Emailing attached files can be complicated, especially when three or more people are all modifying the document. If all collaborate using one document, you save time, make collaboration more direct and precise, and make it easier to track who contributed what. Changes appear in colored text, and users are emailed when someone edits the document.

The most popular wiki is Wikipedia (www.wikipedia.org), an online encyclopedia that has become the largest encyclopedia in the world and operates without an editorial staff (Tapscott & Williams, 2008). Wikipedia has thousands of volunteer writers and editors who have collaborated using Web 2.0 technology to create the available information.

Wikispaces

Wikispaces (www.wikispaces.com) is a tool for creating and managing a wiki that advertises itself as "the world's easiest wiki solution." When you create an account on Wikispaces, you will be asked if you want to create a wiki and if you want it protected. You may click in a list that allows you to open your wiki to everyone on the Internet worldwide (who can then edit and contribute to it), allow everyone to view it but only members to make changes, or make it private so that only invited members can view and edit it. Once you log in to Wikispaces and create your wiki, simply click New Page to create your wiki page. A word processing–style window will appear with all of the font and formatting buttons you are accustomed to using in a program such as Microsoft Word. When you are finished with the document, you simply save the changes by clicking Save at the top. Each person in your group also will be able to edit and create pages for the wiki—freely if your wiki is open or at your invitation if you have made your wiki private.

When you are working in your wiki, you will see several tabs across the top of the webpage. Click on the Discussion tab to participate in threaded discussions with your group members. This might be where you discuss why you made changes to the document, coordinate how you want to proceed on the project, or share ideas by interacting with other group members. The History tab allows you to revert to previous drafts of the wiki page. Wikispaces allows you to create multiple pages for a wiki, each with the Discussion and History functions.

Teachers can use Wikispaces to have students collaborate, a particularly useful function for group and class projects. Wikis provide an environment for students to solve problems together, even collaborating with a class in another country. Administrators can use Wikispaces to collaborate on projects with colleagues to build a curriculum, develop district or building policies, write grants, or support an event. Professional learning communities, personal learning networks, and communities of practice collaborate to develop improved teaching strategies, create authentic assessments, and build a knowledge repository.

Google Documents

Google Documents (www.docs.google.com), known as Google Docs, is another web-based document sharing tool. Unlike a wiki, which is a collaborative webpage, Google Docs takes the place of software such as Microsoft Office for generating word-processing documents and spreadsheets.

The Google Docs software is used online rather than by opening a program on your computer. This is commonly referred to as residing *in the cloud*. In other words, the Google Documents are saved on the web, where they can be accessed by anyone and from any computer. Keeping your document in the cloud has benefits. For example, if you would like to work on a project from multiple computers, you do not need to carry a USB flash drive around with you. With Google Docs, you can access the document from anywhere simply by logging in to Google. This also eliminates the possibility of losing your file, should your computer crash or should you lose your USB flash drive.

When you create a Google Doc, the only person who can view and edit it at first is you. However, you can share your Google Docs with as many as two hundred collaborators. Collaborators use their Google log-ins to access the document once you have shared it. Collaborators then are able to add content to the document, revise it, and add comments. Google Docs saves versions of the document before each collaborator makes changes to enable you to revert to a previous draft if you disagree with a collaborator's revisions.

Google Docs makes collaborating much simpler than emailing a Word, Excel, or PowerPoint document to your collaborators, which allow only one person to make changes to the document at a time. With Google Docs, collaborators can make changes simultaneously—try it to share your next project.

Use your Google account (if you set up Google Reader discussed earlier in this chapter, you already have one) to create and manage Google Docs. Using Google Docs is much like working in Microsoft Word or Excel. When you log in, a screen appears that allows you to open a document. You have options to create a new document, select a document you already have created, select a document someone shared with you, or upload a document you started in Microsoft Office. Once you have selected an option, a word-processing (or spreadsheet or slideshow) screen appears with familiar formatting and editing tools (font, formatting, spell check, and more). As you work in the document, your work is saved automatically. To share a document, click Share on the top right corner of the screen, and enter your collaborators' email addresses.

Practice by choosing a Word, Excel, or PowerPoint file you are currently working on. Upload the document to Google Docs and experiment with making changes. Remember, when you want to send the document to another user, click Share rather than emailing it. Consider using Google Docs to create a curriculum or budget, or for any project that requires collaboration.

Tools for Social Networking

There are plenty of tools online to build and nurture your personal learning network. Here are some social networking tools that will be practical and valuable for you and your students.

Ning

Ning (www.ning.com) might be for you. Are you part of a special interest group who would like to connect online, but you don't have the web-development skills to set up your own website? Then, Ning *is* for you.

Most are familiar with online social networks such as MySpace or Facebook, but thousands of niche social networks have been designed for people with specific interests. For example, online social networks can help you find your next job, help you parent—or help you as an educator. Ning is a powerful tool that allows anyone to create a specialized online social network for a few dollars a month. Social networks on Ning can feature discussion forums, blogs, photo and video sharing, widgets from other websites (small representations of applications that you put on a webpage for specific information or functionality, similar to apps for smartphones) such as Google and Twitter, and an RSS reader to share blog feeds from outside of Ning (such as your Edublog feed).

You may want to consider joining a few Ning social networks before you create your own so you get a feel for how people connect, interact, and collaborate.

Classroom 2.0

Classroom 2.0 (www.classroom20.com) is good place to start. The Classroom 2.0 Ning social network is comprised of nearly fifty-eight thousand educators interested in using Web 2.0 in education.

You can use Ning to create a network for faculty, staff, alumni, students, and parents to interact. To set up a Ning site, create an account at www.ning.com, and you will have an option to create a network. The site will guide you through the process of selecting a name and web address for your network, as well as selecting a layout, color, and design theme for the network's features (for example, where on the page you want features such as the discussion section, blog section, or photos and videos to appear). Once you make selections, you will be able to launch your own social network. You can invite people to your social network by clicking on the Invite tab, where you type in names and email addresses along with text for the invitation.

When you launch your network, you will see your network page with a series of tabs for maintaining it. The Manage tab takes you to a page with settings for your network that you can use to further customize the network.

Tools for Extending Learning in the Classroom

Free and useful online tools are plentiful for extending learning outside the classroom. Here are some resources that may be handy for you and your students.

Video: TeacherTube

TeacherTube (www.teachertube.com) is an online community for sharing educational videos made for teachers by teachers. TeacherTube has many of the same features as YouTube, yet the content is tailored to educators.

The TeacherTube community offers a selection of videos, from interviews with veterans to an overview of the periodic table to an explanation of Web 2.0. The instructional videos posted on TeacherTube may allow you to expand your professional knowledge by learning from other educators or may be suggested to students to watch at home or in the classroom. While the videos on TeacherTube are popular, the site also is an online community for hosting discussion forums and sharing documents, photos and visuals, blogs, and audio. Teachers uploading information to share have made TeacherTube a vibrant professional learning community.

TeacherTube looks and feels a lot like YouTube and is easy to navigate and use. You can search for videos, documents, visuals, and audio by using keywords. Like YouTube, after you view a video, you can leave comments and rate its quality. Feedback is important, because it helps community members identify the most useful videos from the thousands available. Consider searching TeacherTube if you are researching a new educational topic or if you would like to add audiovisuals to a presentation, meeting, or lesson plan. You can post links to the material on your blogs, wikis, Twitter profiles, and Ning networks. If you have content you think the TeacherTube community would find useful, you can select Upload to share it.

Real-Time Updates: Netvibes

Netvibes (www.netvibes.com) is an all-in-one dashboard to collect everything that's happening now on your social web. It offers an efficient way to stay current while managing the vast amount of content uploaded to the web each day. Using Netvibes, you can view real-time web updates all on one page on the content you find useful or interesting. You can use a template or create a completely customized page and fill it with selected widgets. You can find a widget on Netvibes for just about anything, as most major web applications and websites have widgets. You also can create and share the dashboard with your personal learning community.

With Netvibes, you can create a personal dashboard in just a few minutes and instantly access current information about selected topics whenever you open your browser. The most difficult task is deciding which widgets to put where on the screen.

Once you log on to your Netvibes account, choose from widgets such as to-do lists, blog feeds, news, shopping, weather, or other categories. You also can find widgets for many of the tools described in this chapter (such as Delicious, Twitter, and Google Docs). You can add these widgets, arrange them on the page, and select a background image and color scheme.

You can use multiple pages to set up your Netvibes dashboard, represented as tabs in the horizontal navigation bar. You may want to set up a homepage tab with the most pertinent widgets, followed by more specialized tabs with widgets such as a productivity tab, with to-do lists and calendar widgets, and an education tab, with education-related news and blogs.

Managing Your Online Reputation

In today's connected world, reputation management is an important skill. You are defined by what appears on Google, Yahoo, and Bing. A quick google of your name can be telling. In fact, some companies are making a profit at helping folks "scrub" their online mistakes. However, a better way to approach reputation management is to proactively build your digital footprint, making sure your attempts at transparency do not go awry. Connected educators google well.

As you become comfortable with the idea of authoring and posting content online, you will need to create a plan for making sure the information that remains connected to your name online is all positive.

According to a Pew study (Madden, Fox, Smith, & Vitak, 2007), nearly half of all Internet users (47 percent) have searched for information about themselves online, up from just 22 percent in 2002. Younger users (under the age of 50) are more prone to self-searching than those 50 and older. Men and women search for information about themselves in equal numbers, but those with higher levels of education and income are considerably more likely to monitor their online identities using a search engine.

How does one manage their online reputation? How do you create a positive digital footprint on the web?

Your digital footprint is a collection of the activities and behaviors that are recorded while you interact in online spaces. Everything you post is recorded, for the most part. The trick is to take control of your footprint in such a way that when you are searched for online, the content you want affiliated with your name turns up in the search.

Here are some tips for managing your online reputation.

- **Build your own professional webpage or blog:** Include your contact information, specialty, and curriculum vitae, as well as some work samples. Share your ideas related to your philosophy of education.

- **Stack the deck in your favor:** Use services like Google and LinkedIn to build information about yourself through online profiles. You want to have several profiles that a search engine can pull from so that those searching for you will be able to distinguish between you and another individual with your name.

- **Share your insights:** Posting your thoughts and ideas on blogs as comments or authoring online articles in your area of expertise is a smart way to reinforce your professional reputation. Be visible in positive ways.

- **Be professional at all times:** If you regularly contribute to blogs or forums, give thought as to how your statements may be interpreted. Mentally editing yourself should become regular practice. Ask yourself, would I say this or post this picture if my mother was looking over my shoulder?

- **Track yourself:** Using Google Alerts (www.google.com/alerts), analytics, and other services to alert you when your name is used in online spaces can help you be proactive in managing the way you are perceived online.

Where Are We?

It will take time to become familiar with all of the tools discussed in this chapter and the opportunities to share, connect, and collaborate with connected learners worldwide. Eventually you should be able to connect the concepts of learning communities to the practical applications presented.

Where to Now?

In chapter 6, we move on to the specifics of organizing a community, that is, building and extending your personal learning network. We also will look at suggestions for facilitating learning and finding balance in a connected learner model.

Get Connected

Join us on Diigo at www.diigo.com/tag/clc-tools to view all of the links discussed in this chapter as well as additional tools that support connecting and collaborating. Add some links to your own Diigo bookmarks.

Chapter Six

Building Your Connected Learning Community

Do not go where the path may lead; go instead where there is no path and leave a trail.

—Ralph Waldo Emerson

Our Stories

My first memories of building a personal learning network go back to the early 1990s. I had just gotten online and started using bulletin boards to find people with whom to learn. My first attempt was on a science board called Newton. Amazingly, it still exists as of writing this book (www.newton.dep.anl.gov).

The first person I met on Newton was a young science teacher who taught me how to use IRC chat and how to share files and have private conversations. We shared information about science education and weather. He even tutored some of the children in the charter school I was leading. Through email and a bulletin board system, I added a second network member, a fellow university professor I had never met who was from a department other than education. We used a threaded discussion format to talk about education and what needed to change. It was the first time I connected with someone I didn't know, who felt exactly like I did about kids and learning.

Another connection was with a government employee in Edmonton, Canada, the first international relationship I had ever had. We experimented with tools and technology ideas, and we discussed politics. We sent artifacts to one another trying to learn about each other's culture. He sent me an Oilers hockey puck and jersey and a videocassette of his family playing in the snow. Today, I not only have hundreds of Canadians in my personal learning network, but I have visited Edmonton and even played in that snow myself.

It all started through my conversations with someone who, at the time, seemed so different from me but who now, through the connections I have in the network, doesn't seem very different at all.

—Sheryl

In these times of constantly changing, ever-increasing information, it is impossible for any individual to access, much less know, everything. Instead, knowledge, learning, and innovation can be managed within virtual networks and communities and then leveraged to amplify learning for all.

Journalist Steven Johnson (2008) writes in *The Invention of Air*:

> Ideas are situated in another kind of environment as well: the information network. Theoretically, it is possible to imagine good ideas happening in a vacuum. . . . But most important ideas enter the pantheon because they circulate. And the flow is two-way: the ideas happen in the first place because they are triggered by other people's ideas. (p. 51)

Personal learning networks help you leverage deeper connections and relationships, and from those networked relationships, you grow a community of connected learners and leaders. Through the additional connections and memberships in connected learning communities, professional growth is deeper and more profound, and learners are more capable of sustaining authentic change. Personal learning networks make that two-way flow happen, and the result is deeper learning.

A personal learning network "involves an individual's topic-oriented goal, a set of practices or techniques aimed at attracting or organizing a variety of relevant content sources, which are selected for their value, to help the owner accomplish a professional goal or personal interest" (Warlick, 2007). *Networks are about the individual.* They consist of streams of people, information, expertise, learning objects, and images that are of interest to you.

Networks are where you find ideas and information to bring back to your existing communities (professional learning communities and communities of practice) to develop into programs, to use to create action research, and to implement in your schools. Out of these network connections you also find people with whom to grow ideas and start new collaborative projects. Networks are about what *you* want to learn. Communities are about the collective *us* and what *we* are building or improving on together, systemically. The potential for your network to help you learn lies in its diversity, the quality of relationships, your ability to filter well, and your willingness to give as well as take.

It's tempting and easy to allow online spaces like Twitter, Flickr, and other social networks to become one big link-sharing party. But the real power of the social web is revealed when you have a plan and a purpose for how you'll build your network, reap its benefits, and then apply the knowledge you gain.

Starting Your Personal Learning Network

What do you want to accomplish or learn from your personal learning network? Where do you begin to build? How do you attract the right people and organize the relevant content? First, remember that networked learning is personal, so adapt and remix these suggestions to fit your goals and experiences. Second, growing a personal learning network takes time, effort, and perseverance. Remember to take the posture of a learner. You will grow as you go.

Begin with the tool of your choice, and add others as you feel comfortable. A number of tools can help: blogs, RSS aggregators (such as Google Reader, Bloglines), Twitter, social bookmarks (such as Delicious and Diigo), archiving and note-taking software (such as Evernote), photo sharing (such as Flickr), and electronic mailing lists. Don't be too concerned about the tool names; they will change over the years. Think instead about the outcomes and what you want to use the tool for. Choosing the right tool for the job is important, like having the right tool for building or transporting something in your physical realm. If you are just beginning your network, begin slowly, with one task and tool, then try another and another. Contrary to what many techno-enthusiasts believe, he who has the most tools does not win.

Tips for Getting Started Online

- Establish one consistent username across all networks to build and manage your online reputation and identity.
- Find a mentor, if possible, to help you on your way.
- Choose those you respect, see who they follow, and select your first connections from their list.

Decide Whom to Follow

Who you follow depends a great deal on the purpose or focus of your network. You'll get the most value from filtering (choosing and vetting) your connections. You can find potential participants in many places.

Borrow From Bloggers

You may want to begin your network by considering well-respected bloggers with whom you are familiar. Often bloggers include links to their Delicious and Twitter accounts. Review who is in their networks and whom they read and follow.

As you build your network through blogs, Delicious, or Twitter, include people from diverse backgrounds and perspectives, as that dissonance will extend your learning. In each case, before you add a person to your network, review that individual's profile, his or her blog or website, and the content that person has shared, be it a blog post, a resource on Delicious, or a number of tweets on Twitter.

Use Twitter Lists

Another way to get started (be sure you're signed in) is to visit the Twitter account of a person who matches your interests. On his or her profile page, Twitter will list other users who are similar. For example, the list Solution Tree Authors will have not only us, but others who write about educational issues who are worth following.

You also can use a site such as the Twitter4Teachers wiki (http://twitter4teachers .pbworks.com) to help you find and vet people to follow and to advertise yourself so people have the opportunity to follow you. Interestingly, Twitter4Teachers began as one teacher's attempt to organize and recommend the people in her own Twitter network. It has since grown as people from around the world have found the site and added their own Twitter names.

Vet Before You Follow

How do you decide whom to trust? One strategy we use is to do a web background check before we choose to follow someone. We research a person's digital footprint. Questions we ask are:

- "Does this person use a real name or some pseudonym like @bikinigirl?" We only follow those who use their real names in connection with their accounts.
- "Is there a website in the profile? Does this person blog?"
- "How many tweets has this person made, and are they of value?"
- "When was the last time this person tweeted?"
- "Are we interested in what this person is sharing?"

We pay a great deal of attention to people's digital footprints and how they manage their online reputations. We never follow someone in return just because that person chose to follow us. We make conscious decisions about who the person is and why he or she fits into our personal learning goals and should become part of our PLN.

Use Social Bookmarking

Delicious and Diigo both allow you to build a network around content. You connect to people who are linking to or bookmarking the same things you are. Check who has a particular person in their network. One of the great features of the network is that people you respect will do the vetting for you—just look at who they choose to follow.

Nurturing Your Personal Learning Network

Growing and nurturing a network means engaging in conversations in safe, ethical ways. Through ongoing and reciprocal sharing, you develop relationships, and the possibilities for learning expand. The network becomes more significant as relationships grow. As Martin Weller (2009) states:

> It is when an element of reciprocity is added over the blanket sharing that the network attains a more significant role in your life. Sharing is to reciprocity as gold-mining is to jewelry making—the latter cannot exist without the former, but it is the latter which adds real value and interpretation.

Putting It in Practice—In the Classroom

When Karl Fisch (@karlfisch), an educator at Arapahoe High School in Littleton, Colorado, learned he would be teaching a section of algebra in 2010–2011, he turned to his personal learning network as he planned lessons and assessments.

On his blog, The Fischbowl (http://thefischbowl.blogspot.com), the first post in which he shared his intent to crowdsource his planning garnered twenty-two comments (Fisch, 2010). In posts that followed, Karl's personal learning network responded to his requests for ideas on assessment, parent communication, writing, and expectations. Karl has reciprocated by providing a window to his classroom in posts his personal learning network can learn from (Fisch, 2011).

How many network connections should you try to maintain simultaneously? Different experts offer different answers. Some research suggests that an individual cannot maintain a stable social relationship with more than 150 people at one time (Dunbar's Number, 2011). Will Richardson, Sheryl's partner at Powerful Learning Practice, uses this number to guide his network choices and keeps to that number, deleting some connections if necessary. He carefully chooses whom he will learn from on Twitter based on diversity, alignment with his personal interests, and time. Sheryl, however, believes the larger the network the better, thinking that networking is more about connections than deep, stable relationships. For Sheryl's Twitter followers who are new to Twitter and just beginning to build their networks, she feels that nurturing these newbies to the social web is an important part of her online participation. Sheryl views the data as a river of information constantly flowing by and admits she has never read every post that her network offered in a given day. She plucks one or two links out of the steady stream of ideas to bookmark in Delicious. Other days she will wade in the Twitter river a little deeper, spending an hour or so reading, replying, and gathering ideas. Typically she checks the feed in the morning by sharing links to articles she is reading, and she might check back in the evening to see if anyone found one of her posts useful and retweeted it. Retweeting affirms that she is adding value to her network.

Both approaches—limited and unlimited contacts—have value. Choose the approach most suited to you. To reach its greatest potential, however, a personal learning network requires attention. Over time, like tending a garden, you will reap its rewards.

Putting It in Practice—In the School

Noah, a high school administrator, started growing his learning network by reading educators' blogs. Noah chose blogs from those suggested in a session at a regional educational technology conference; his friends recommended others. He used an RSS aggregator to pull the blog content into one place for easy access. He participated in conversations on the blog, commenting on the posts he read or adding links and relevant resources.

Over time, Noah's comments began to show more of his own voice, and other blog commenters mentioned how his ideas added depth to the conversations on the blog. He decided to blog on his own, becoming a producer of ideas rather than just a consumer. As he began to share his thinking on his own blog, Noah realized that he was growing in ways that commenting on others' blogs had not allowed. In addition, the excitement of getting comments from others around the world motivated him to go deeper and post more often. He was not only growing as a blogger, he was growing his own readership, a readership that was sharing links and resources with him, as he had done when he was just a commenter.

One resource Noah used was Delicious, the social bookmarking tool (described in chapter 5) that allowed him not only to save bookmarks but to build a network of individuals who were saving things that also interested him. His networking toolbox for building his personal learning network was growing. Gradually, adding not only resources but also people to his growing network, Noah figured out the best ways to filter the stream of information coming to him. Finally, he created an account at the microblogging site Twitter, and using a vetting process, started adding people whose interests matched his own to his network. You may choose to begin with a different tool than Noah; what's important is that you begin.

A Word of Caution

Many online learners prefer networks on Twitter or other electronic spaces where they can share short conversations and where their ideas are met by like-minded support. The advantages of networking are many, but personal learning networks are only one of the three prongs necessary to be a do-it-yourself learner in today's world. For all the positive connections, links, and ideas that networks offer, they are only a part of what is needed for lasting change.

Networks expose you to provocative ideas and people that you likely would not have found in your local professional learning community or your global (but still relatively small) community of practice. If chosen carefully, these networks stretch and diversify your learning and thought processes and help you grow. Personal learning networks provide sources of new information that give you just the right amount of cognitive dissonance and friction to produce new ideas that, when you bring them back to your local community, become innovations. Networks provide breadth. Communities provide depth.

Networks are just the place to connect, share resources, meet others, and get inspired. They're great for self-directed learning, but are very *me* centered in that *we* choose our mentors, feeds, resources, learning objects, and those with whom we learn. Networks feed our need to be in control. We can be very visible and yet still passive, never having to put ideas into action. If all we do is network, then we miss the opportunity to go deep in a collaborative environment and produce something that will support change. As our colleague Nancy White says, it is from networks that communities form or fall. It takes both networks and community to become a connected agent of change.

Think About

What are you doing to cultivate your personal learning network? Have you taken the first step? Are you both giving and taking in your networked relationships? What strategies have worked for you in building your network connections?

Designing Your Connected Community

Professional development in the 21st century can be do-it-yourself—based on your needs, interests, and passions. As a reminder, connected learning communities are a three-pronged approach to effective professional development using the local (professional learning community), contextual (personal learning network), and global (community of practice) environments. Most importantly, we hope you understand that to shift from a classroom framework of teaching to a community of co-learners, you must see yourself as a *learner first and a teacher second*. This three-pronged approach to do-it-yourself professional development produces global learners who share, apply, and synthesize what they learn in order to improve.

However, the burning question is how to design a connected learning community that is compelling enough to successfully compete for the attention of busy educators or students, particularly those in your own school or district. Because communities are voluntary, to succeed over time, they need to generate some excitement, add relevance, and bring members value.

What contributes to a community's ability to engage participants? Figure 6.1 (page 98) shows the characteristics of a healthy community. It lists those traits that, based on our experience, help engage others in knowledge sharing. In planning a community, you could build an action plan around each of these aspects.

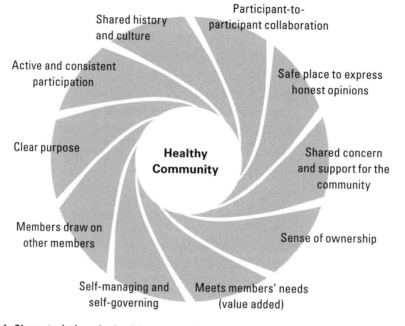

Figure 6.1: Characteristics of a healthy community.

Here are some guiding questions as you plan your community.

- How do we design supports to sustain healthy online communities of practice?
- What strategies enable these characteristics to emerge and evolve?
- What design elements foster a connected learning community?
- How quickly do we encourage the community to become self-managing?
- What is the purpose of our community?
- Do we want a closed or open community?

To build for knowledge *of* practice, as defined in chapter 3, we need to design a community in which members engage in activity and discussions, help one another, and share information. The community is united not just by shared interests but also by practice (Wenger, 1998). Connected learners find that sharing, mutual inquiry, and action research can lead to increased student learning. In community, we problem solve and reflect, building our capacity for change and influencing policy (Costa, 2007).

Designers face a balancing act between allowing the community to develop organically through viral interaction and intentionally structuring growth through an embedded design. The design needs to allow users to build trust, generate enthusiasm, and exchange ideas, yet not create so many options that the learning curve overwhelms and frustrates users, causing them to leave.

Remember, as you create a design, that teachers new to virtual learning communities crave structure and familiarity. Rather than having a lot of options, most teachers are used to a linear experience in traditional classrooms or system-offered professional development. Online experiences produce more nonlinear outcomes, and our observation is that once the initial excitement of receiving a reply to a post wears off, educators are easily overwhelmed. Too many choices of communication tools or too much prepared content can confuse people. As one new member commented in November 2008 just two weeks after joining a private social networking community:

> Hmmmm . . . still working this out. I haven't participated as much as I should have and this could be part of the problem. It also seems as though there is very little structure to all of this. Great if I was certain about where this was all going, not so great when you're in the dark about a lot of things.

On the other hand, participants need choice to actively engage and to co-create content, or the virtual community is doomed in its first few weeks. For example, in two communities of practice created by large, well-known technology companies, the viral impact was diminished because the companies controlled the content during the first few months. The designers, trying to model *best practice*, limited people's posts to certain categories and handpicked contributors to share content in order to build the quality of what was shared. In the process, members lost ownership. Those who joined had few options to contribute or to have a vested stake in the conversations, and so participants never established a sense of community. What might have been a vibrant discussion and resource-rich venue resulted in nothing more than a collaborative blog in an underused community space.

Early Facilitation

We have concluded from experience leading thousands of educators in purposeful communities that in the early stages of community building, the founding members should create the features they would like to see incorporated into the community design. We ask members, "What have you found valuable in the communities to which you belong? What keeps you coming back?" The diversity of participants' culture and ideology helps create a learning space that is more versatile than what designers alone could imagine. In addition, both novice and experienced users can incorporate design elements that meet their needs. With the purpose of the community in mind, users develop a shared vision of what the community will become. As the core members create content together, they begin to build a common understanding of what niche the community fills and how it will function.

The community then begins to create a historical context and shared history. The core participants begin to recognize what it means to be a member of this community and can then recruit others. Community founders will have had a clear mission in mind, but we recommend allowing a flexible design to accommodate the group's emerging needs. Designers should integrate what they learn from users to help the community evolve in healthy ways.

In healthy communities, participants discover how to leverage members' collective intelligence. They understand what each member knows and start to generalize much of the explicit and tacit knowledge into mentoring experiences or changed classroom practice. Important shifts occur, from *what you know* to *who you know*, and then from *who you know* to what *who you know* knows. The value is in understanding how to tap into and leverage others' knowledge and experience once you figure out what fellow community members know.

Figure 6.2 illustrates the evolving features of an online community and suggests what to expect as the community grows and prospers.

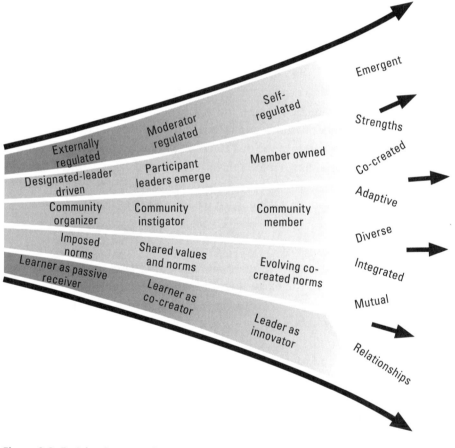

Figure 6.2: Evolving features of a healthy community.

Table 6.1, which summarizes the evolutionary stages of community life, can be helpful in designing new communities.

Table 6.1: Design Model for Evolution

Conception and Launch	Emergent Design	Engagement	Active Community	Adaptive Shift
1. Community founders conduct focus groups and needs surveys on design and functionality. 2. Founders announce effort to establish a community. 3. Community founders help bring educators to community. 4. Community members determine purpose and style (open or closed). 5. Community members establish loose governance and identify community leader.	1. Community begins to build shared vision and design. 2. Community founders introduce simple framework of collaborative tools, including profile tools for connecting. 3. Founders offer multiple options for giving feedback on design and tools. 4. Members develop a sense of trust and community through co-creation of content opportunities.	1. Community values social and cognitive presence of formal community leader. 2. Community begins to establish patterns of interactivity. 3. Viral impact becomes evident in membership (if open). 4. Community members determine design improvements based on experience, resulting in changed processes.	1. Natural community leaders emerge. 2. Community becomes more self-regulating and self-governing. 3. Community demonstrates benefits from collective work and collaboration. 4. Community forms various subgroups based on interests and passions. 5. Community engages in inquiry and begins to create solutions and innovations.	1. Designers use participants' ideas and innovations to reconceptualize and redesign. 2. Developers rethink (unlearn) structured and programmatic uses of community, challenging their own assumptions about innovation. 3. Members sponsor and mentor the development of new communities around innovation.

Think About

What is your purpose in developing a community? Which items in table 6.1 are most useful to you?

Roles and Responsibilities

David Lee was inspired to create the 4L Model (Lee, 2006) after reading an interview with digital culture expert John Seely Brown (Conner, 2000). Lee's model describes the roles and interactions that members of an online community adopt. Lee says that, community members self-select their roles based on their participation—and may adopt more than one role depending on the conversation. Lee (2006) explains the roles as:

1. **Linking**—These educators might be interested in joining the community; they visit occasionally and harvest links.

2. **Lurking**—These are legitimate peripheral participants. They are reluctant to share their thoughts and ideas transparently, but they are willing to listen and watch from the sidelines.

3. **Learning**—Community members who frequent and participate in the community's life are learning. They bring to the group as much as they take from the learning experience. They help shape what the collective is gaining.

4. **Leading**—These educators commit time and energy to the community. Leaders may emerge organically from the community or be identified at the launch as leaders.

Effective connected learning community members, who are learning and leading, should make it a goal—of any community design—to draw those linking and lurking participants into the action.

Since 2004, we have experimented with a variety of roles and structures in the online communities and initiatives we've led. In sizeable, highly active communities with a continuum of learning goals and a significant lifespan, we've had the most success in sustaining engagement by layering our support—that is, creating a community support group made up of individuals with varying degrees of time commitment and leadership responsibility who serve as team leaders, community organizers, connected coaches, or expert voices. They are all fellow educators who help see the work through and make certain that community members are engaged and active. Table 6.2 summarizes these roles and structures. These are just examples; communities could develop and use a host of other roles.

In addition to the roles outlined in table 6.2, various roles and responsibilities emerge from community members' special experiences or interests. For example, if you notice a community member is particularly good at nurturing new members, create a title for the role such as *greeter*, and put that person in charge of it. Maybe you have someone who loves adding research articles to the conversations as a way of supporting another's point; create a title for that task, and put that person in charge of it. Empower your members to find others to help them carry out the roles. Let members figure out what works as they define the role. Learn from their strengths.

Table 6.2: Sample Roles and Structures in Successful Connected Learning Communities

Role	Function	Relevance to Community
Participant or team member	General member or user in the community	Participates because it's essential to community's life
Team leader	Participates regularly as team member	Develops skills needed to lead a professional learning team online and develops a professional learning community in the local, face-to-face context
	Facilitates and encourages	
	Acts as day-to-day liaison between school and the community design staff	Is organized around team project goals
Fellow or coach	Helps lead and moderate discussions in the online community	Provides support to entire community but usually assigned to two teams to specifically provide virtual support and encouragement
	Starts and extends discussions, shares resources, and offers support	Engages as a participant in deepening his or her own knowledge and in creating learning contracts, action research, or technology-integrated lessons plans
		Builds capacity in assigned team leaders and team members
Expert voice	Facilitates subgroup discussion around particular topics	Links members to vetted voices outside the community and connects them with subject-matter experts on as-needed basis
	Models personal learning network development	Offers unique perspective on discussions and shares resources
		Focuses on helping participants build their own personal learning networks
Community leader	Oversees cohort community and supports participants and various leaders	Helps all community members become active participants
		Works behind the scenes to support socializing, relationship building, trust building
		Provides stimulating material for conversations, keeps the space organized, helps hold members accountable to the stated community guidelines, rules, or norms
		Builds capacity in fellows, coaches, and team leaders
Community organizer	Creates community sites, wikis, and the community brand	Fosters leader interaction, provides stimulating material for conversations in leader subgroups, helps hold leaders accountable for meeting the stated community guidelines, rules, or norms
	Posts initial content and answers all trouble-shooting questions concerning the platform	
	Trains and encourages community leaders	Builds a shared culture by passing on community history and rituals

Support Builds Buy-In

I have been inspired by the exchanges with our experienced voice leaders. [The experiences they] have described in great detail are the kinds of things I'd like to facilitate with my students. . . . I've joined the Global Education Collaboration and some others that I learned about through my groups. . . . I'm just a hair away from some of this with our kids. And I'm confident that with the tools and connections I'm making through our Ning and the support of our experienced voices I'll get there . . . and most importantly . . . my students will get there! They have provided me with the sites and organizations to take what I have done with students to an entirely new level.

—*Mary Pat Harris, Milford, Ohio (as cited in Ritter-Hall, 2010)*

Evolving Your Community

Here are some useful tips to use as guideposts as you build and evolve connected learning communities. They have been extrapolated from the many lessons we have learned along the way from our own community experiences.

Put People Before Things (or Test Scores)

When people are asked to challenge the status quo, engage in mutual accountability, change to match job descriptions, and develop new skills, they become unsettled and resistant. Focus on the people, not the tools, in your networks and communities, and while your interactions with them and expectations of them play out in an online community, remember it is a *human* community. Relationships matter. Be patient and respectful, and treat people in your online networks who are struggling with change with the same kindness you would give to people in your everyday world.

Design With Real Learning in Mind

Community and network connections should have a purpose beyond sociability and the harvesting of links. Any group of folks having professional conversations on Facebook or Google+ will say they learn amazing things from each other. But do they really? Or are they just experiencing the euphoria of knocking down classroom walls and eliminating the silos teachers have been trapped in for years and years?

Through communities and networks, educators have found each other, and now they are using social media as the new space for their electronic teacher's lounge—they are giddy with the excitement of sociability and sharing cool stuff. But how many educators who've joined the social media revolution are really leveraging their Twitter networks and Facebook connections as a means to intentionally affect the culture of their schools and districts or to fundamentally change the learning environment for students? Successful connected learning communities harvest links and *do* something with them. They revisit the ideas shared in a hashtag-driven Twitter chat and work together to make thinking explicit. They challenge assumptions and build shared knowledge.

Design your community with an intense passion and serious commitment to question the status quo (no matter what the consequence) so real learning happens. We need fierce resolve to keep at it and see it through past the storming, all the way to performing, where transformation is business as usual and deep learning is the norm (see page 67).

Design for Evolution and Loose Governance

As you develop your tribe on and offline, do you understand how to make the most of the skills, experiences, and wisdom in your group? Distributed leadership brings everyone to the leadership table (students too) and allows them to be the CEO of something. The trick is finding out what that something is exactly. Look to your community members' passions. What are they good at? What do they know a lot about? Leaders should see themselves as capacity builders who care as much about helping teachers self-actualize as they do students. When students have self-actualized teachers, they soar.

Communities should begin with loose governance and a plan to evolve. Loose governance will allow for an easier launch and more comfortable experience. However, as members become more experienced with collaborating in your community space, let the community evolve based on members' needs and strengths. Avoid a rigid design and governance that does not allow active member involvement and leadership. Participants want to add to the community and need you to create opportunities for buy in and co-ownership. Community leaders need to be working hard toward shifting the leadership to the emerging leaders within your community. Model yourselves out of a job, and have the action groups talk to each other and share what they are learning.

Select a Passionate Community Leader

Even with loose governance, the community leader or organizer can make or break the community. This person needs to have an established digital footprint, a discernible online voice, and a personality that pulls people into conversations. The leader needs to be genuine, a good facilitator, and able to infer what is *not* being said in posts. This person needs to be able to understand that deep relationships *can* be developed in online spaces. This person knows how to ask great questions that energize members and deepen the work. Community leaders share content, but they also are adept at pulling content from others. They work to make members visible while making themselves less visible. They understand how to celebrate small accomplishments and are comfortable using social media to share and reflect transparently.

If you do not have the resources to hire a community leader, grow one from within the community. We have seen schools share the role of community leader, rotating leadership roles monthly. Another idea is to divide the leader role into multiple, smaller roles that teacher leaders in the community perform. You could try guest leadership, bringing in a well-known community leader or networker who volunteers the time to support your cause. Parents, retired teachers, graduate students, and other nonschool staff may have time to take on a community leadership role.

Co-Create the Content

If only the leader is sharing content, not all community members' needs are likely to be met. When other members share, more of them are likely to find the content of value. When all members are deciding where and what they will read, do, or reflect on, real action and learning take place. Make it as easy as possible for natural leaders to emerge. Learning communities thrive when they are built on collaborative action and co-created content. Smart community designers will use such content-development strategies as action research (see chapter 7, page 113), shared document development, group blogging, and more to help members develop a sense of ownership for the community.

Bring in Other Voices

Bringing in guests who have name recognition adds to your community's appeal. The community's excitement about collaborating with leaders creates a desire to participate. Invite recognized names to join in your activities, and empower them to lead or create while they are with you. School-based learning communities should leverage their local connections. Have your superintendent be a guest for a week. Invite an author or other subject matter expert. Pull in folks from your personal learning networks to share their expertise.

Build Trust

In a face-to-face environment, multiple cues—facial expressions, body language, voice intonation, and quantity of interactions—help build trust naturally over time. In online spaces, building trust requires developing profiles, identity tools, and forum discussions meant specifically to create a sense of community. If you base these digital experiences on face-to-face trust-building activities, you will ensure that members come to trust one another.

Remember that technology is an amplifier that can accelerate more students and teachers toward wider understanding and deeper learning. Technology is not an elixir. It isn't a silver bullet. Technology *is* a great tool for connecting folks and providing powerful spaces for meaningful global collaboration. However, learning transforms us and our students, not the tools. The magic of your community space is not in the tools—the blogs, wikis, and podcasts you include. Those mediums should be invisible and secondary to the learning, sharing, and co-construction that happen in those spaces. In building a physical structure, we do not focus on the hammer or nails, but on what we can build with the hammer and the value of what will transpire inside that space once we've created it.

We used to sit kids in front of a computer and have learners interact with learning objects contained within the software programs. Now we have learners sit at a computer and see it as a portal they pass through to connect with great minds and other eager learners from around the world. The connected educator is always asking, "Who can we learn from today? What will we build together?"

Think About

In organizing for community, which areas will be most challenging? What roles and responsibilities will you use? Will your community be open or closed?

Where Are We?

- A personal learning network becomes an *outboard brain*, a source of collective intelligence, as a result of the connections in that network.

- A personal learning network takes time and perseverance but is worth the effort.

- Basic tools can help build a personal learning network, including deciding how to select participants. Nurturing the network is important.

- A healthy community is based on a good design for learning and on content co-creation.

- Communities evolve from conception to launch to shifting as they adapt to user needs.

- Community members have roles and responsibilities—linking, lurking, learning, and leading—and those roles evolve over time.

- Members must learn to balance time and priorities while adding the richness that connected learning brings.

Where to Now?

It is time to engage in connected learning if you have not. For those who have experienced the potential of connected learning, this is the time to renew your commitment. Jump in and engage with others; add your gifts and your talents to collective wisdom. Grow and nurture a personal learning network; leverage your network's wisdom and use an online community of practice to strengthen your local professional learning community. Create a connected learning community. Build your own passion-driven education. In chapter 7, we explore ways to keep that excitement alive and growing.

Get Connected

1. Create a Twitter account at http://twitter.com, and follow at least ten people. Use the information in this chapter to decide who you will follow.

2. Need help with Twitter? Visit http://support.twitter.com for support.

3. Follow Lani at http://twitter.com/lanihall

4. Follow Sheryl at http://twitter.com/snbeach

5. Post something on Twitter using the #connectedlearner hashtag.

Chapter Seven

Sustaining the Momentum

Much like a movie projector on a screen, human systems are forever projecting ahead of themselves a horizon of expectation (in their talk in the hallways, in the metaphors and language they use) that brings the future powerfully into the present as a mobilizing agent. To inquire in ways that serve to refashion anticipatory reality—especially the artful creation of positive imagery on a collective basis—may be the most prolific thing any inquiry can do.

—James Cooperrider, professor of
organizational behavior,
Case Western Reserve University

Our Stories

In a community that started in February 2011, conversations slowed. Within the fellows subgroup, Cary wondered if we were losing momentum. At a colleague's suggestion, she raised her concern with the full community in a discussion post titled "The Lurking Cave." That one post garnered ninety-three responses, many from members who had rarely participated in discussions. It was the sixth–most popular conversation in the community and surfaced periodically for over two months. That one post initiated a voyage of discovery for the community—re-energizing many participants, providing a new eye on a familiar landscape for others, and illuminating the previously hidden fears of reluctant members.

Empathy and passion emanated from the community in words of encouragement and support for doubters. Cary's initial passion for engaging the community sparked the interest of others, who repeatedly invited everyone into the conversation; along the way, many adopted a new lens on learning within community.

At my computer, my smile broadened—emerging leaders, new eyes on learning, momentum regained—and for the moment, our community was vibrant and flourishing.

—Lani

What if you work and prepare, but nobody shows up for your network? Or worse, people show up, look around, decide it isn't worth their time, and leave! Some might think developing a virtual learning community is easy. After all, it's virtual—nobody even has to worry about what to wear! Creating a connected learning community, however, takes know-how. Sustaining that initial momentum is even harder.

Learning communities, like gardens, flourish when they are cultivated, when they are nourished as they evolve and mature. Neglected or taken for granted, they languish, losing their splendor and appeal. As gardens need a gardener's expertise to flourish, a community needs a leader. Communities of practice are generative, and that capacity thrives when a leader continually redesigns and develops the community. Gardens and communities continually grow and have to be rethought in order to meet the needs of the practice and to maintain the community's vigor. Unfortunately, there is no algorithm for this work. Communities need members who have the capacity to be adaptive (A. Hargreaves, 2004). A key group emerges as the community finds its rhythm. According to Bolam, McMahon, Stoll, Thomas, and Wallace (2005):

> Sustaining change requires: sustaining deep learning; involving a broad range of people in "chains of influence"; spreading improvements . . . ; it being done on existing resources, not through special projects where the funding then dries up; nourishing and taking care of people, rather than burning them out; sharing responsibility; activist engagement to secure outside support. (pp. 26–27)

Appreciative inquiry and action research are two strategies that will help engage network participants and keep them involved to sustain the change. In addition, perspectives on scale can guide our work for change through connected learning. Finally, using an implementation map (an innovation configuration) will help members gauge where they are along the continuum of putting the innovation into practice.

Appreciative Inquiry

Appreciative inquiry is a valuable approach to sustaining learning and change in communities and networks (Cooperrider, 1996). In appreciative inquiry, learners work from a "what if?," or strengths, perspective rather than a deficit perspective (finding a problem to fix or a gap to address). Transforming what people think is at the forefront of our actions (Bushe & Kassam, 2005). In this approach, inquiry is "appreciative, applicable, provocative, and collaborative" (Seel, 2008a). In appreciative inquiry, community members acknowledge and explore others' ideas and ask provocative questions to see where their conversation will take them.

Putting It in Practice—In the Classroom

This exchange inside a community of practice models appreciative inquiry. Lani was coaching Courtney, a teacher.

Courtney: *Almost every day of my teaching career my students teach me a lesson. This is the most recent. This year I was fortunate enough to have a small group of my ELL seniors in a class where the primary focus was "success," whatever that happens to look like; our focus was "college-bound." We spent the year on the Free Application for Federal Student Aid, college applications, college visits, scholarship applications, Accuplacers, college essays, and a number of other activities. We also formed a club called ELL STARS, which stands for English Language Learner Seniors Trying and Reaching Success. We worked many events, did tons of community service hours, and bonded as a group. As we headed into the end of the year, our focus turned to college acceptances, graduation, and how to spend the money the group had raised. We started the year saying that our money would go for a junior scholarship, a senior gift back to the ELL department, and the remainder for a senior trip. About two weeks ago, a member of this class was diagnosed with kidney failure. The students and I were floored. On their own, they placed jars around town to raise money for this student and then voted to give all the money we had worked so hard for to their friend to help him get his kidney transplant. I was reminded, as I am every time I am taught a lesson, that sometimes school is not about the lesson, the curriculum, the discipline, the classroom management. . . . Sometimes, it's just about the kids! As I think about these students, the word "success" shows a new face! They are there; they are a success!*

Lani: *What I hear you saying is, it is about the kids—dealing with great challenges, dealing with success—it is about them, who they are and what they can do. I've got that right, don't I? How does that then influence what you do in your classroom, now and in the future?*

Courtney: *You have it right! It's just a reminder to me that taking time every day to get to know your students a little better is what will help when students experience those really rough areas in their life that tend to draw them down the wrong paths—the paths that lead to discipline issues, or truancy, or really bad decisions. It's during these times that relationships can pull a student back onto the forward-moving path.*

Appreciative inquiry is based on a number of assumptions and principles. The assumptions are:

- In every group or community, something is working.

- What people focus on becomes their reality.

- Asking good, generative questions influences people.

- Groups and communities are more comfortable with change when some things that work don't change.

- Language creates reality.

- Recognizing differences is of value (Hammond, n.d.).

The principles are:

- What we concentrate on develops into our reality.

- Appreciative inquiry is positive and supportive.

- Change and inquiry are simultaneous.

- Embracing the power of stories changes members' thoughts.

- How we behave and think is affected by how we anticipate the future (Seel, 2008b).

A number of appreciative inquiry frameworks exist. One is the 4-D model (Cooperrider, 1996; Cooperrider & Whitney, 2005), shown in figure 7.1. The inquiry begins with *discover*, moves to *dream*, and goes on to *design* and *destiny*.

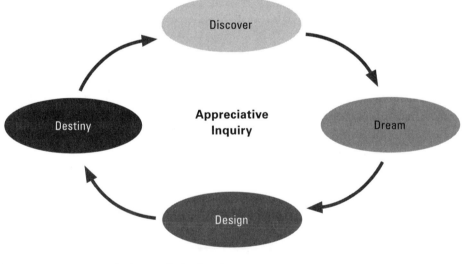

Figure 7.1: The 4-D model of appreciative inquiry.

1. **Discover:** People share stories with one another that illustrate when they feel the group or community is at its best.

2. **Dream:** The entire community envisions the future as if the high points members found in *discover* are not extraordinary but everyday occurrences.

3. **Design:** The community creates a design for the organization based on the *dream* stage.

4. **Destiny:** The community implements the changes.

The cycle highlights the positive, generative perspective of appreciative inquiry. Shared stories become the basis for envisioning the future; from that vision, the team creates a plan, which, when implemented, allows the community to move forward. The appreciative inquiry continuously cycles. Using an appreciative lens is one way for communities and organizations to keep momentum.

Action Research

Action research is typically performed in a school setting; however, for a connected learning community, it also works well within online communities of practice. Action research is a collaborative activity among committed colleagues looking for answers to everyday, real problems related to classroom instruction, systemic change, or a more global issue. Action research is learning by doing; it allows practitioners to examine and address issues over which they can exert some influence (Ferrance, 2000).

Typical steps in the action research process are:

1. Identify an issue or possibility.

2. Gather data and information about the issue or possibility (both within the local context and from what others looking at this issue have done).

3. Interpret the collected data and develop an intervention or initiative to address the issue or possibility.

4. Collect data and artifacts after implementing the intervention to determine whether it succeeded.

5. Begin the cycle again.

What groups learn from their action research can be applied in collaborative planning to build momentum for more positive change. The action research gives the professional learning community a purpose for working together toward a common goal. Action research projects may be the first time teachers have collected data, made inferences about the data, and then used their ideas to take ownership of a problem they have collectively identified and are trying to solve. The process can be empowering and transformational.

Dave Dale, a Canadian science teacher, reflected on his collaborative action research experience:

> I was involved in another action research project that also had to do with 21st century learning, but this one was focused on classroom implementation. My group decided to work on building staff capacity. We surveyed our staff to determine a baseline comfort and ability level within our building. From our results, we built an Edmodo site for our school. We built the site with two goals: helping people to build personal learning networks, and as a repository for resources and group knowledge.
>
> This project is far from complete. As a group, we need to continue to drive this project within the building. We need to keep adding people to our own networks and helping our likeminded colleagues to build their networks. We need to get people talking about the benefits of having a personal learning network in order to help us convince the more reluctant people on staff to join us. We need to convince our administrators to use the site as a communication tool with the staff. We need to connect educators from all over the world to our site and share their insights and ideas with our staff. In case it hasn't come across in the simple text on the white page, I am very excited to help others learn some of the things that I have learned this year. It was a very steep learning curve, and I had to confront some preconceived notions of my own. (D. Dale, personal communication, May 15, 2011)

Action research often is tied to what happens in the classroom and often begins with a series of questions. Danielle Cripe, an Ohio teacher, posted this on a blog about her personal learning community's action research project:

> What does it mean to be an inventive thinker? Are our students inventive thinkers? If not, how can we get them there? Is our definition of a creative, inventive thinker different than that of the students?
>
> These are just a few of the questions discussed by my group prior to presenting our findings. After months of preparation, experimentation, and discussion, our findings were pretty interesting. (Cripe's Chronicles, 2010)

Think About

Which strategies (appreciative inquiry and collaborative action research) will you use to keep momentum going?

An Ohio Team's Action Research Project

Danielle Cripe and her team from the Forest Hills School District in Ohio transparently chronicled their action research around developing inventive thinkers. They shared their abstract, the problem they faced, and their objectives and assessment so others could learn from them.

Abstract

Inventive thinking in the 21st century requires that students be self-directed and curious and possess sound reasoning. Five middle school teachers designed individual units of instruction that focused on developing inventive thinkers. The academic subjects represented were social studies, language arts, and science. Results showed three themes in each of the units of instruction: (1) authentic tasks, (2) student ownership, and (3) connected learning. Student, teacher, and community feedback was collected, as well as student work samples.

Problem, Issue, or Possibility

The problem we faced was a misconception of what inventive thinking looked like in a classroom. We thought inventive thinking could only be used by a small percentage of the student population, as most students didn't know how to or even want to invent new solutions to problems. We also questioned whether middle school students were capable of inventive thinking across academic disciplines.

Objectives and Assessment

We initially wrestled with four questions: What is inventive thinking? What does the teacher do in a classroom where inventive thinking is occurring? What does the student do? How do we know when a student is inventively thinking?

We needed a model to design units of instruction and decided to use problem-based learning to aid in unit development. We collected student, teacher, and community feedback, and also collected student work samples (Cripe, Kelly, Moore, Place, & Preston, 2011).

Scaling Up

Most of us have been involved in projects in which scale was focused only on increasing the number of participants or in which scale was viewed as separate from sustainability. Coburn (2003) advances a model that highlights the complexity of scale, saying that transformational change requires simultaneous attention and focus to four elements: (1) depth, (2) sustainability, (3) spread, and (4) shift. These areas provide the momentum your work needs to move forward. (For an example of scaling up, see appendix B, page 163.)

Depth

Depth refers to a change in practice that has meaningful results. It refers to altering "teachers' beliefs, norms of social interaction, and pedagogical principles as enacted in the curriculum" (Coburn, 2003, p. 4). Depth is not only about teacher or leader action but also about an educator's underlying beliefs about learning. Depth encompasses what students, teachers, and parents hear in conversations with leaders and teachers. Depth is about changing the design of learning experiences for staff and students. *To achieve scale in the dimension of depth, your project or initiative should have caused transformational changes in practice.*

Putting It in Practice—In the School

A team of educators at Trevor Day School in New York City initiated an action research project while immersed in an online community of practice. Their questions were:

- How do we use experiential learning and community values to extend our school's mission and create 21st century educators and learners?

- How can we create a learning environment that promotes 21st century skills in support of Education for Sustainability? (Education for Sustainability is a dynamic system of core content, competencies, and habits of mind coupled with a pedagogical system that is learner centered and inquiry based.)

In a two-year professional development plan, the school's educators created a grid to display lessons across the two dimensions on which they focused; the team evaluated lessons within the framework of the Education for Sustainability standards and 21st century skills and helped teachers create new coursework that met the criteria. In the second year, the entire faculty participated in the evaluation process and created new lessons that met their objectives (Schecter et al., 2011).

Sustainability

Sustainability is maintaining meaningful, profound changes over substantial periods. Coburn notes that there is "ample evidence that sustainability may be the central challenge of bringing reforms to scale" (Coburn, 2003, p. 6). She suggests that reform efforts, if they are to scale, must be sustained with integrity beyond the initial period.

Achieving depth is significant in helping sustain innovation. When teachers change their beliefs due to an innovation, they are more likely to remain true to the reform effort despite changes in leadership or diminishing resources. Innovations that receive widespread support are also more likely to be sustained, a fact that accentuates the need for policies that promote collaboration. Sustaining scaled growth means that the initiative has stood the test of time, even against negative changes in context, such as economic downturn or political change.

Spread

Spread is typically viewed as additional numbers of buildings, teachers, or classrooms involved in the reform effort. Coburn, however, views spread more inclusively, extending it to "reform norms, beliefs, and principles within schools and districts" (Coburn, 2003, p. 5). This lens reinforces the importance of reculturing, which embeds the norms of the innovation into supportive policies. Knowledgeable and supportive district and community leaders are also needed for the reform effort to be scaled up. Achieving scale within the area of spread means that the project is extended to more people while using the same amount of resources and maintaining the same level of quality and effectiveness.

Shift

Finally, scale is comprised of an element of shift—a shift in the ownership of the reform effort. Often those outside the community or district may initiate or administer the effort—for example, an external professional development provider initiating a reform or a funding organization administering a grant. Community, district, building, or teacher ownership is critical to scale. Ownership involves a commitment to the innovation, to its spread, depth, and sustainability. Shift then can involve developing capacity for ongoing professional development to maintain the integrity of the initial reform effort. Shift is necessary for the reform to spread and be sustained when different priorities arise, funding is lost, or policies fail to support the initiative. To achieve full-scale shift, the innovation must be co-owned, co-assessed, and co-designed.

Evolution

Dede and Rockman (2007) suggest a fifth dimension of scale: evolution. Evolution means adapting and revising the initial effort. If the adaptations and revisions are significant, designers may rethink the change effort—thus the evolution. Others' adaptations of the work teach the project designer something that causes the designer to change the design.

Think About

Consider the connected learning communities in which you invest time. In what ways can the idea of scale inform your planning for projects that improve student learning? How can you and your professional learning community use scale to improve? How do you take your best ideas, your early successes, and your islands of promising practice to scale?

Assessment and Evaluation

How can connected learners assess our efforts and evaluate our participation? How can we judge the effects of the change we work for? Formal and informal instruments are available, but we will focus on the informal ones. The Concerns-Based Adoption Model (CBAM) is a basis for informal ways of assessing progress in both local and global communities.

CBAM Informal Assessments

Locally, fifteen-minute walkthroughs provide a picture of the effect of a professional learning community's efforts to improve instruction and learning and to encourage reflective practice. Walkthroughs involve a protocol: they do not interrupt instruction; they provide teachers with feedback; and they allow teachers to discuss opportunities for additional improvement (Hord & Sommers, 2008). Members who travel the online community can virtually implement walkthroughs, checking its health and progress. After a virtual walkthrough, the group may provide all members with feedback through a discussion and seek the community's input for moving forward.

In addition to walkthroughs, Hall and Hord (2006) find that one-legged interviews are helpful in determining how a new effort is proceeding. One-legged interviews are informal interviews that can occur in the hallway, the staffroom, or the cafeteria with individuals or small groups. They last no longer than a person comfortably could stand on one leg. With a few succinct questions, members' views on community processes become clearer. The interview responses can help move communities forward.

In communities, understanding members' concerns about a reform effort or new practice can lead to conversations that clarify, help, and guide those who are not comfortable with the innovations. Hall and Hord (2006) and Hall and Loucks (1979) have identified seven stages of concern that individuals facing change may feel.

1.   **Awareness:** Educator has little concern about or interest in the innovation.

2.   **Informational:** Educator expresses a general interest and wants to know more.

3.   **Personal:** Educator wants to understand how the reform effort will affect him or her.

4.   **Management:** Educator focuses on tasks, information, and processes.

5.   **Consequence:** Educator is concerned about the reform's impact on students.

6.   **Collaboration:** Educator collaborates with others to enact the reform.

7. **Refocusing:** Educator, energized by the benefits, begins to brainstorm and imagine strategies for remixing and improving the reform effort.

Members' responses to the open-ended question, What concerns do you have? can suggest ways to move forward.

Hall and Hord (2006) and Hall and Loucks (1979) also have delineated eight levels of use to help community members identify the level at which a new practice is being implemented. The stages of concern focus on affective aspects of change; the levels of use explore members' behavior with regard to the reform. Members pass through the sequence as they adopt a new practice or reform.

1. **Nonuse:** No action taken, no interest

2. **Orientation:** Gathering information

3. **Preparation:** Planning ways to incorporate

4. **Mechanics:** Concerned with mechanics

5. **Routine:** Implementing with comfort

6. **Refinement:** Looking at ways to improve

7. **Integration:** Collaborating with others; integrating into other uses

8. **Renewal:** Investigating new innovative ways to implement

Imagine an interview question to the members of your local or global communities that seeks their feedback on what they are doing in terms of the new practice or reform effort. When the feedback is analyzed through the lens of the levels of use, that information can become a foundation that assists others in moving through the sequence of implementation. While the stages of concern and the levels of use identify individual concerns and use, the innovation configuration identifies what comprises the new practice or reform effort. The innovation configuration, created before implementing an innovation, presents a picture—what the innovation looks like in practice, what students or teachers will be doing—in a two-dimensional rubric. Components that describe the intended outcomes are listed vertically; these outcomes must be observable and show what the practice looks like if fully implemented. A horizontal list of variations describes various phases of implementation, from nonuse to fully implemented (Newhouse, 2001). The map provides a clear goal for all.

For example, a group of likeminded educators come together to create an online community in which they plan to collectively explore more about how emerging, social web technologies change learning. As a group, they decide to create an innovation configuration map that describes their vision of the community at various levels of implementation (ideal, acceptable, or unacceptable actions), as illustrated in table 7.1 (page 120). The map describes the components of the community and various levels of implementation built on the characteristics of a healthy community from figure 6.2 (page 100).

Table 7.1: Online Community Innovation Configuration Map

Outcomes	Levels of Implementation		
	Ideal	Acceptable	Unacceptable
Participant-to-participant communication	Members engage with each other—respond to each other's ideas in posts, comment on each other's videos and photos, and post comments on each other's pages.	Approximately 40 percent of members communicate with each other. There are also communications between the community organizer and members.	Members fail to communicate with each other. Contributions to the community are lacking.
Safe place to express honest opinions	Members with diverse perspectives transparently and actively share opinions and ideas, which are accepted, built on, or challenged through civil discourse.	Members respond to ideas that differ from their own. There are times when those responses push the limits of civil discourse.	Members express reluctance to share honest opinions, and difficult conversations fail to occur.
Sense of ownership	Members often provide feedback on the direction of the community and support each other in responses as they engage in difficult conversations.	Members provide feedback on the direction of the community when asked. Some members support others in difficult conversations.	Members do not provide feedback nor do they engage in conversations around difficult topics.
Meets members' needs	Members add value through the co-construction of knowledge around the focus of the community and initiate conversations.	Although some members do not engage in conversations, co-construction of knowledge occurs among a core of members.	Members rarely participate in co-construction of knowledge or initiate conversations.
Self-managing and self-governing	Members develop norms for the community and reprimand other members if those norms are challenged.	Members come to consensus on norms for the community and name a group to monitor community interactions.	The community organizer creates and enforces rules with no input from members.

Outcomes	Ideal	Acceptable	Unacceptable
Members draw in other members	Members, on their own, encourage others with common interests to join the community and also invite those on the periphery to engage more.	Whenever a request is made of community members, they reach out to others to join the community. A group of members seeks participation from those on the periphery.	Members take no action to pull others into the community.
Clear purpose	The community purpose is clearly stated, and there is no question that the activity of the community aligns with its mission of exploring how emerging, social web technologies change learning.	The community purpose is stated and the community, for the most part, maintains its focus on its mission of exploring how emerging, social web technologies change learning.	The community purpose is not stated, and the activity of the community has no focus.
Active and consistent participation	Members participate on a regular basis with meaningful contributions to which others reply.	Members participate on a regular basis.	Members participate very little.
Shared history	The shared history is honored and carried forward as the community continues to improve practice and co-construct knowledge.	The practice in the community is shared and builds on the co-construction of knowledge that has come before it.	Members disregard any co-construction of knowledge that precedes their participation.
Shared concern and support for the community	Members continually work together to bring energy and innovation (events, webinars, new ideas, experts, and new members) to the community.	When the community is challenged by discord, lack of focus, or stagnancy, leaders emerge from the members to collectively resolve varied issues.	Members engage in discord and make no attempt to resolve issues.

Think About

How might these strategies be of value in assessing your own collaborative learning community?

Path Markers for Connected Learners

Connected learning paths are dynamic, organic, personal, and self-directed, and—stretched over varied networks and communities—they represent a huge landscape. Table 7.2 suggests path markers that have guided many in becoming more connected learners. You may want to remix or adapt these for your personal learning, then share transparently with all of us in our connected learning community.

Table 7.2: Path Markers for Connected Learning

Disposition of a Connected Learner	Path Markers
Is a co-learner, co-creator, and co-leader	**Innovative:** Is a leader in collaboratively researching, designing, and developing ideas for new practices **Collaborative:** Collaborates in co-creating knowledge with members of professional learning community, personal learning network, and community of practice (that is, a *connected learning community*) **Routine:** Adopts a learning posture and accesses resources from personal learning network and communities
Is self-directed	**Innovative:** Creates new avenues for learning and collaboration and shares them with others **Collaborative:** Takes the initiative for activities that promote team and community learning and moves past cooperative activities **Routine:** Locates resources and initiates opportunities for cooperative learning
Is open-minded	**Innovative:** Crafts opportunities for collaboration to resolve differences and develop understanding; demonstrates a willingness to consider implementation of alternate ideology **Collaborative:** Strives to understand the perspectives of team and community members; listens actively **Routine:** Tolerates different perspectives
Is transparent in thinking	**Innovative:** Actively works to involve others in collaborative activities to generate transparent thinking through intentional modeling; takes risks in modeling transparent thinking

Disposition of a Connected Learner	Path Markers
	Collaborative: Participates in team and community conversations **Routine:** Shares thoughts on blogs and in blog comments
Is dedicated to the ongoing development of expertise	**Innovative:** Embraces a leadership role in developing expertise for a collective practice **Collaborative:** Works with the team and community to develop a more accomplished collective practice **Routine:** Works continuously to improve personal practice
Commits to deep reflection	**Innovative:** Establishes unique strategies and activities to enhance and encourage reflection that results in collective-efficacy building **Collaborative:** Reflects collaboratively with the team and community **Routine:** Reflects frequently in his or her blog
Engages in inquiry	**Innovative:** Takes a leadership role in collaborative inquiry to realize more accomplished collective practice **Collaborative:** Inquires with the team and community to resolve and improve problematic areas of practice **Routine:** Asks questions and seeks answers to personal and professional dilemmas
Values and engages in a culture of collegiality	**Innovative:** Opens deep conversations around practice that leverage the wisdom of other connected learners to design innovative practices; serves in a curator role by connecting great ideas to one another **Collaborative:** Believes none of us is as good as all of us; initiates collaboration around problems and issues **Routine:** Engages in and values conversations around practice in teams and communities
Shares and contributes	**Innovative:** Begins and extends conversations around difficult topics, leverages knowledge construction across networks and communities, and is viewed as a thought leader **Collaborative:** Regularly collaborates and contributes thoughts, ideas, and resources to local and global teams and communities through discussions, podcasts, images, and videos **Routine:** Shares resources and routinely connects with personal learning network (local and global colleagues)

continued →

Disposition of a Connected Learner	Path Markers
Commits to understanding gained by listening and asking good questions	**Innovative:** Seeks to promote knowledge of practice by beginning discussions that encourage teams and communities to dig deeper and ask questions to realize systemic change; encourages debate of ideas **Collaborative:** Asks questions of teams and communities to deepen personal understanding **Routine:** Listens to understand
Explores ideas and concepts, rethinks, revises, and continuously repacks and unpacks, resisting urges to finish prematurely	**Innovative:** Leads difficult discussions and encourages others to persevere and to continue reworking ideas for authentic change in a collective practice **Collaborative:** Participates in ongoing team and community exchange of ideas **Routine:** Is inquisitive as ideas are explored and re-examined for personal practice
Exhibits courage and initiative to engage in discussions on difficult topics	**Innovative:** Brings difficult topics to communities with an appreciative mindset and moderates the subsequent discussions; is always mindful of the possibilities **Collaborative:** On teams and in communities, participates and supports others in conversations **Routine:** Adds personal perspective to discussions
Engages in strengths-based appreciative approaches	**Innovative:** Leads an initiative for change from a strengths-based approach **Collaborative:** Celebrates the unique strengths of team and community colleagues and highlights the possibilities that arise from their collective strengths **Routine:** Reflects on strengths and considers possibilities
Demonstrates mindfulness	**Innovative:** Creates and facilitates opportunities for educators to collaborate in a nonjudgmental, purposeful space **Collaborative:** Collaborates on teams and in communities nonjudgmentally **Routine:** Approaches learning purposefully
Displays willingness to experiment with new strategies	**Innovative:** Suggests new practice to improve student learning; responds to others' requests for testing of and feedback on practices they view as promising; takes risks with new ideas **Collaborative:** Adopts new practices from team and community for personal practice and transparently shares experience **Routine:** Explores new practices

Think About

Which of these path markers will guide you as a connected learner? Which do you see as most challenging? Where would you put yourself on each of these on a scale from innovative to collaborative to routine?

Where Are We?

- Sustaining a community is continuous, hard, and rewarding work.

- Leaders ensure that the community continues to grow and stay active. Leaders should also recognize the importance of nurturing new leadership.

- As participants' knowledge grows through collaboration, they should work together to identify and address neglected areas of practice.

- Communities are part of an ongoing cycle of evolution, cocreation of knowledge, and community building.

- The ideal model is appreciative inquiry, which focuses on changing what people do rather than transforming what people think. A 4-D model of appreciative inquiry includes: discover, dream, design, and destiny.

- Coburn's model of scale highlights four dimensions: depth, sustainability, spread, and shift.

- Evaluation and assessment play roles in developing and sustaining community.

- Path markers for connected learners are not linear. They are dynamic, organic, personal, and self-directed.

Where to Now?

In whatever your role—teacher, librarian, leader, or other educational specialist—you are now investing in and becoming or growing as a connected learner. Chapter 8 discusses the concept of not only learning through collaboration but also leading. What impact might distributed leadership have in a connected learner model? The possibilities and potential are great when the voices and gifts of formal leaders, teachers, and students join to create systemic, authentic change.

Get Connected

1. Develop your own Edublog. Register by going to http://edublogs.org /signup and filling out the form.

2. View the guides under the Getting Started section on the Edublogs site.

3. Make sure to record your blog URL, username, and password in a secure place so that you can access it later.

4. Write a blog post about creating a personal learning network, your proposed community of practice, and your personal learning community in your school. What are some steps for development or things to consider? Visit http://bit.ly/eH1i1x if you need help writing your first post.

5. Publish the post. Congratulations, you are now a blogger!

Chapter Eight

Transforming Leadership for a Connected World

We must start by disposing of our old assumptions about leadership and about who can lead. We have placed too much responsibility and too much power with the few individuals whom we label "leaders" in our school systems. Superintendents, curriculum directors, and principals cannot on their own generate leadership that improves education.

—Gordon Donaldson,
professor of education,
University of Maine

Our Stories

I was at a teaching fair in Valdosta, Georgia, applying for my first teaching job. In an interview, I explained how I wanted to change education and what my classroom would look like. The interviewer paused and said, "Can I tell you something off the record?" He said no principal would hire me. Shocked, I asked why. I had been a top student and the darling of my education classes. Surely I would be hired. "Principals want teachers who follow the rules," the interviewer said. "They want teachers who are 'yes' men, teachers who will carry out the mandated curriculum. Not visionaries who want to change education." I was shocked and dismayed at his words, but he was right.

Few schools have distributed leadership models where teacher leaders are free of standardized agendas and able to create a system that allows kids to solve challenging problems around topics about which they and their teachers are passionate.

Fortunately, later I had Greg Anderson as my principal while I was taking on a coaching role. Greg understood capacity building and empowered the teachers with whom I worked to make decisions, important decisions that impacted kids and the school as a whole. He encouraged us to create out-of-classroom initiatives for kids. He coached me as I developed a new curriculum to reach our most at-risk learners in a school that served the city's largest population of homeless children.

A busy administrator, Greg did not have time to design or lead a new approach with our lowest-scoring kids, nor did he have time to get the buy-in and commitment to learning something new from a group of already overwhelmed teachers. But because he valued distributed leadership and trusted teachers, he knew that together, as leaders, the teachers were much better than any of us could be alone.

—Sheryl

Formal leadership is typically associated with position and role-based power. Traditionally, formal leaders have led in sometimes authoritative ways: Do what I say because I told you to, and I will give you a paycheck. Leaders led, others followed. Transformational leaders, in contrast, are collaborative decision makers who empower stakeholders to actively participate in learning and leading. Transformational leaders encourage collaboration through the lenses of connected learning and distributed leadership.

Transformational leadership involves us changing our working relationships and shifting our mindsets. Transformational leaders understand that leading is a shared responsibility, and that the greater the investment in staff talents and expertise, the greater the return. This view of leading as a shared relationship involves shared purpose, action, and responsibility, and a reorganization of power and authority (Apple & Beane, 1999; Frost & Durrant, 2003; Fullan, 2002). It aligns capacity building with democratic ideals. Capacity building and self-actualization become as important as student achievement.

"Leadership capacity," according to Lambert's definition, "refers to broad-based, skillful involvement in the work of leadership" (1998, p. 3), suggesting that teacher leaders and student leaders, as well as those in positions of formal leadership, all may be involved in leading.

Distributed leadership "involves the leadership functions of a school being shared by many people in ways that strengthen the whole school community, intensifying a sense of engagement and shared responsibility," according to Greg Whitby (2006, p. 2), executive director of schools for the Catholic Diocese of Parramatta, Sydney, Australia. Everyone is a co-learner, co-leader, and co-constructor of knowledge in the best interests of students.

The shift to distributed leadership can be difficult. Traditional leaders must reconsider concepts of control and power. As leadership is redefined and boundaries blur, the essential question becomes, what can we do together to move forward?

Transforming Systems

Kilgore and Reynolds (2011), in *From Silos to Systems: Reframing Schools for Success*, suggest that leaders use a distributed leadership model organized around action teams of faculty representing the school, parents, and students to solve problems and remove obstacles to learning based on an area of focus, such as curriculum, technology, or professional development. Using the lens of connected learners, curriculum action team members, for example, would follow thought leaders on Twitter whose passion is curriculum. The technology staff would read blogs of thought leaders in technology. Each action team would not only have the knowledge of its own professional learning teams but would use connectivity to gather global expertise to inform ideas, projects, and problems.

The chairperson of each action team would be part of a guiding coalition reporting to school leadership about the teams' efforts and accomplishments. The guiding coalition would keep schedules from colliding and would communicate so that everyone stayed informed. Each action team would understand the work and tasks of the others and how they sync their efforts systemwide.

All the action teams would come together in an online space (community of practice) where they would share and reflect about the processes, challenges, and work flow they each were experiencing in their professional learning communities. The knowledge gained from the transparent and deep sharing in this space would help each action team improve over time and ensure strong, coordinated collaboration across the system.

Transforming the Principal's Role

Principals as transformational leaders take the posture of learners themselves. They model becoming connected. They share their role authority, and they empower those with whom they work.

Transformational principals relinquish control and encourage the development of collaborative relationships (Harris, 2003). Donaldson (2007) notes, "Great schools grow when educators understand that the power of their leadership lies in the strength of their relationships. Strong leadership in schools results from the participation of many people, each leading in his or her own way" (p. 29). Principals who understand how important it is for leaders to also take the posture of a learner develop leaders who more easily model and demonstrate respect, fairness, and equality and act as gate-openers to change.

Transformational principals *connect*. They are highly visible models for leading professional learning communities, using personal learning networks, and nurturing communities of practice. They learn and practice reputation management and model this strategy for faculty. They blog and know how to build a readership that supports school initiatives. They use their Twitter accounts for positive school public relations and social media to involve stakeholders in celebrating student work and faculty achievement. Connected leaders understand how to leverage social technologies to promote a culture of learning and promote open leadership and school transformation.

The goal for those in positions of formal leadership is to make certain that supports outweigh the challenges for teachers to become leaders. Distributed leadership changes the principal's role from school manager to capacity builder. They involve others in decision making. They ask teachers to take on important tasks, rather than delegating, and rotate responsibilities among staff members. They are interested in the self-actualization and professional growth of teachers as well as student achievement.

Connected principals cultivate connected teachers as leaders. Understanding the special qualities that excellent teachers possess—knowledge of children and subject matter, empathy, dedication, persistence, technique, sensitivity to communities and families, readiness to help, team spirit, and ability to communicate—is an essential component of school leadership that a well-developed network can strengthen. By building relationships, principals can identify individual teachers' strengths and gain valuable insights into how to leverage those strengths for the good of the whole. Novices often have expertise and experience with using technology or social media, for example. Wise administrators leverage that knowledge by allowing these tech-savvy beginning teachers to lead workshops and initiatives aimed at producing connected learners in the school. By allowing new teachers to lead from their places of power early on, principals nurture the teachers' self-efficacy and strengthen their personal power. Investing in the school's social fabric pays off for the school as a whole.

Putting It in Practice—In the School

George Couros is passionate about distributed leadership. As the principal of Forest Green School and Connections for Learning in Stony Plain, Alberta, Canada, George believes that a collaborative environment that includes all stakeholders will help ensure that all children's needs are met: "I know that as principal, I am only a part of the learning process, and I work hard to give everyone the opportunities to become leaders in our school community" (Couros, n.d.).

In George's school, teachers become leaders in professional learning communities. George gives teams a time and a place to collaborate. Several staff members have leadership positions at the schools. Students lead assemblies. Parents and staff work together to create shared visions for the schools:

> *If all of us work together as a school community where we all have the opportunity to share our strengths and become leaders, the limits of what we can do are endless. In fact, together we can definitely change the traditional definition in society on what a true leader should be. (Couros, 2010)*
>
> Follow George on Twitter @gcouros and The Connected Principal blog (http://georgecouros.ca/blog).

Think About

In your district or building, is the concept of distributed leadership a stretch? If you are a teacher, has your administration ever tapped your talents for leadership? If you are a leader, are you aware of faculty members' strengths and talents?

Transforming the Teacher's Role

Transformational leadership in the 21st century means redefining teachers as full-fledged leaders. In the past, teacher ideas and expertise often have been ignored as potential sources for leading and learning in schools and districts (Berry & TeacherSolutions 2030 Team, 2011; IEL, 2001).

Barth, a strong supporter of teachers as leaders, suggests that "something deep and powerful within school cultures . . . seems to work against teacher leadership" (Barth, 2001b, p. 443). Teachers report that classroom responsibilities and pressure to raise students' standardized test scores deter them from leadership opportunities (Berry & TeacherSolutions, 2011). Some are uncomfortable in leadership roles, reluctant to move outside of their comfort zone in the classroom with children. They may lack the collaboration skills that can help them lead in both offline and online environments. Although teachers are often reflective, they may not be aware of or proficient in the skills needed for collaborative leadership, including asking probing questions, observing and replying without judgment, sharing personal practice and student work, generating new ideas, and challenging others to rethink and remix personal practice.

Yet to adapt to emerging trends in school improvement and accountability, teachers at all levels are assuming greater roles of responsibility and leadership (Berry & TeacherSolutions, 2011; Muijs & Harris, 2003). What does teacher leadership look like? Turning to the literature, we find differences in perceptions.

- Teacher leadership is "the ability to encourage colleagues to change, to do things they wouldn't ordinarily consider without the influence of the leader" (Wasley, 1991, p. 64).

- "Teacher leaders lead within and beyond the classroom, identify with and contribute to a community of teacher learners and leaders; influence others toward improved educational practice; and accept responsibility for achieving the outcomes of their leadership" (Katzenmeyer & Moller, 2009, p. 6). Katzenmeyer and Moller also say teacher leadership roles are as varied as school contexts.

- Teacher leaders are individuals who continuously work on improving their own teaching, provide curriculum development knowledge, participate in school decision making, deliver in-service training for colleagues, and participate in peer evaluation (Gehrke, 1991).

Harris (2002) describes four dimensions of teacher leadership: (1) brokering, (2) participative leadership, (3) mediating, and (4) forging relationships. Through these roles, teachers are able to translate the precepts of school improvement into practice. Other researchers have identified additional facets of the role, including sharing new ideas that affect the school as a whole (Little, 2000).

Teacher leaders are first expert teacher learners who spend the majority of their time in the classroom and take on leadership roles at various times in their careers. When teachers lead in site-based or online professional learning community, schools improve (Katzenmeyer & Moller, 2009). In a distributed leadership model, teachers are learning and leading. Barth notes:

> A powerful relationship exists between learning and leading. . . . This is where teacher leadership intersects with professional development. Teachers who assume responsibility for something they care desperately about—a new pupil-evaluation system, revising the science curriculum, or setting up that computer lab—stand at the gate of profound learning. (Barth, 2000)

Think About

From your perspective as teacher or leader, how can empowering teacher leaders help your district or building meet school improvement goals?

Teacher leadership is not about *power* itself but about mobilizing other teachers' potential to improve student performance. You can be a good classroom teacher, and your students can be top scorers on standardized tests, but you lead only when someone follows. Teacher leadership occurs when a teacher shares *with other teachers* what works (or hasn't worked) in her or his own classroom in an effort to improve performance for all the students in the school.

Teachers lead from places of personal power that result from qualities and skills that make others look to them as leaders (Dana & Yendol-Hoppey, 2008). Some teachers are seen as leaders because of their expertise, or "knowledge power."

Educators with knowledge power are positioned to deepen the work of connected learning communities (Dana & Yendol-Hoppey, 2008). Teacher leaders see the big picture. Those in formal leadership roles give other teacher leaders assigned power by designating roles, such as lead teacher or professional learning community chair or instructional coach (Hunter, Bailey, & Taylor, 1995).

Teachers as learner leaders build collaborative cultures and lead for change. They build on the collective wisdom of the networks and online communities of which they are members, and most importantly, leverage the collective wisdom that passes them in the halls of school every single day.

Empowering Students as Leaders

Distributed leadership is not complete without students as leaders in the school community. For example, in 1993, student researchers at Royal High School in Simi Valley, California, designed and implemented a research project on student opinion that led the school to clarify and redirect restructuring work. The data from the study became part of continuing conversation in the school, students' voices were legitimized, and students engaged in authentic learning that directly affected their future (Shaughnessy & Kushman, 1997). Since that study, educators have been called on to redefine students' role in school improvement programs (Corbett & Wilson, 1995).

Fletcher (2005) says student leadership is a valuable component of education. "Meaningful student involvement," he writes, "is the process of engaging students as partners in every facet of school change for the purpose of strengthening their commitment to education, community and democracy" (p. 5).

Meaningful student leadership is achieved only with careful planning and guidance from connected educators. Adults may resist allowing students a voice in online or offline spaces. Students, too, may be reluctant. And the school culture may impede their involvement. These challenges are not insurmountable. Open discussions, often in online venues, in which students and staff voice opinions can be helpful. And, as with teacher leadership, a culture of collaboration and distributed leadership encourages student voice.

Think About

What can your students bring to the table? How can they help with school improvement?

Setting Policies That Promote Distributed Leadership

Policies at all levels of governance set the stage for increased collaboration and teacher leadership—distributed leadership—to grow and flourish.

Building Level

School leadership can allow professional learning communities to set their own agendas and decide what issues to focus on and what direction to take. Leaders create structures and environments for all stakeholders to communicate and connect with each other virtually and face-to-face, building a sense of collective efficacy and collective action. Collaboration raises the prospect of improving practice and student academic achievement. Various scheduling policies also enable collaboration by creating time (DuFour, DuFour, Eaker, & Many, 2006b) for teams to meet and engage in conversations. Consider the following.

- **Common preparation:** Create a master schedule that includes daily common preparation periods for teams to collaborate, and ensure that teams spend at least one day a week on a collaborative project. This can be tricky, but doable, when building-level teachers are collaborating internationally.

- **Parallel scheduling:** Create a common period for specials in the master schedule to allow teachers across a grade level to meet each day.

- **Adjusted start and end time of contractual day:** Arrange for teams or entire staffs to begin their day earlier or stay later to gain collaborative team time.

- **Shared classes:** Arrange for two teams to combine classes so that while one team teaches, the other collaborates; the teams then swap.

- **Group activities, events, and testing:** Plan group events for students that nonteaching staff can supervise while collaborative teams meet.

- **Banking time:** Shorten teachers' workdays by a few minutes over a period of time and use the accumulated time to allow collaborative teams to meet.

- **In-service and faculty meeting time:** Allow teacher-directed collaboration on staff development days and during designated faculty meetings. Give teachers the freedom to plan what they will do and how they will do it. Accountability can come from finished artifacts rather than seat time in meetings.

District Level

Districts can support building-level changes and also design connected learning communities in which teachers can share their expertise districtwide so that the benefits of their leadership reach more students (Rasberry & Mahajan, 2008). In addition, districts can permit access to social media to extend to stakeholders opportunities to work together in leadership roles for the common good of students.

Adjusting policy to give continuing education credits and step raises for knowledge gained in do-it-yourself professional learning, especially learning in connected learning communities, is another opportunity to support change.

State, Provincial, and Regional Level

A number of state, provincial, or regional policy initiatives can encourage collaboration. Governing bodies might require administrative licensure programs to teach concepts of learning communities and teacher leadership. A multitiered licensure system and pay scale that recognizes teacher leaders would support a shift to distributed leadership. Another approach is to assess administrators on their skills in encouraging collaborative school cultures (Rasberry & Mahajan, 2008), a shift that leads to authentic systemic change, especially when it occurs in a connected space.

In addition, Katzenmeyer and Moller (2009) say that developing teacher leadership should begin in preservice programs. They contend that universities should structure curricular and field experiences to emphasize a teacher's responsibility toward school improvement and should encourage beginning teachers to take limited leadership roles early in their careers in areas where they have personal or knowledge power.

Modeling Connected Leadership

Connected leadership takes the concept of an increased return on investment through distributed leadership to a new level.

Who is a connected leader? You can be—whether you are an administrator, teacher, student, support person, parent, school board member, superintendent, or engaged citizen. That's the reality of today's connected world.

In each of the following scenarios, teachers acted as leaders and connected learners on behalf of students.

Leadership and Learning

Educational thought leaders link leadership and learning, particularly as they occur collectively and within a community.

- Senge (1990b) regards leadership as collective learning, and leaders as responsible for learning. He also states that learning organizations should be "communities of leaders and learners" (Senge, 1997, p. 30).

- Sergiovanni (1992) takes a constructivist view of leadership and learning: "In communities, leadership and learning go together. So does leadership and sense-making" (pp. 40–41).

continued →

- Harris (2003) says that "leadership is part of the interactive process of sense-making and creation of meaning that is continuously engaged in by organizational members. Taking this view, leadership is about learning together and constructing meaning and knowledge collectively and collaboratively" (p. 314).
- Fullan (2002) asserts that learning in context helps produce leaders at many levels within the organization.
- Robertson and Strachan (2001) make the point clear: leaders must also be learners.

Making Time

During the school day, a fifth-grade teacher team struggles to find enough time to plan lessons, reflect on learning, and share resources. The common planning time does not allow time for in-depth planning or for sharing of resources and ideas with the grade-level team. So a connected teacher leader on the team decides to create an online space to help team members collaborate outside of the school day. These teachers use their online community to have the deep conversations missing during their learning day about what works and what is not working in their classrooms. Using collaborative editing tools, they post resources, create lesson plans, and construct other meaningful work. They carry on real-time conversations about grade-level topics. Tools such as Wikispaces, Google Docs, blogs, threaded discussion, and VoiceThread all work to create a shared space.

Becoming a Valuable Team Member

Susan, a new seventh-grade teacher, lacks a solid understanding of her school's curriculum and needs a larger repertoire of instructional strategies that work with seventh graders. Her grade-level team members help when they can, but Susan is frustrated that she cannot contribute as much as she took away. To address the disparity, Susan creates a blog and joins Twitter, important steps in creating her own personal learning network. She begins to gather strategies and resources from others and to contribute her own ideas to her expanding network of educators. She finds that because of the time she invested learning from her network, she has ideas and resources to share with her grade-level team, ideas that she tried in her own classroom and found successful. Susan's personal learning network enables her to build relationships with educators who have similar needs, as well as veteran teachers whose expertise helps her become a stronger teacher. She is both a novice learning from others and a teacher leader who is beginning to lead the way.

Reaching Beyond the School

As the lone music teacher in his school, David finds that opportunities for true collaboration are rare. He participates in a connected learning community, which allows him to integrate into his instruction ideas from colleagues, his network, and a worldwide community of music teachers. David lacks face-to-face personal learning community interactions, but he collaborates with teachers in cyberspace and participates in ongoing, relevant, and meaningful professional learning customized for him. He is able to use that knowledge to enrich his curriculum and the work of his school's core content teachers.

Where Are We?

- Distributed leadership is different from traditional leadership.

- Leadership shared by many people in a school community intensifies engagement and shared responsibility and helps foster a capacity for change and reaching shared goals.

- Adopting a new leadership model requires a shift in mindset and culture.

- Redefining teachers as leaders is crucial. In this shift, teachers resolve common issues through collective brainstorming, have a shared vision, create supportive conditions (sharing time and resources), and are willing to share practice through observations and reflection.

- Empowering students as leaders is important. Student voices add a valuable texture to the social fabric so critical for transforming education.

- Policies can promote system-level collaboration from the building, district, and region to the state.

Think About

Consider the social fabric in your district, building, or community. How can you strengthen the weave and add greater texture to the fabric?

Where to Now?

Tradition says administrators lead, teachers follow. Pam Moran, a distinguished superintendent in Virginia, has heard colleagues define education as "that which transmits forward the status quo." The problem is, in the face of the constant change we are experiencing in today's world, *there is no status quo*. To meet learners' needs, now and in the future, we need to recreate ourselves and rethink how we do our jobs. We need to redefine our actions as teachers or administrators to that of teachers of learning, or learning leaders. In chapter 9, we explore how teachers can remain relevant as we shift to this new way of teaching and learning.

Get Connected

The Teacher Leaders Network, a national initiative of the Center for Teaching Quality, is a network of active communities of accomplished teacher leaders from across the nation. Much of its work is virtual and takes place online.

1. Visit www.teacherleaders.org/featured-bloggers to see the featured blogs on the Teacher Leader Network.

2. View some of the posts, then leave a comment on a post that resonates with you, and introduce yourself as a reader of this book.

3. Use the tag #clc-teacherleader somewhere in the comment you leave.

4. Bookmark the link of the post you commented on on Diigo. Tag the link with #connectededc.

5. See if there are other blog posts with the tag #connectededc on Diigo that other readers of this book have written. Follow them on Diigo.

6. Go to Twitter and tweet a link to your blog post. Use the hashtag #connectededc in your tweet.

Chapter Nine

What the Future Holds

Knowing is not enough; we must apply.
Being willing is not enough; we must do.

—Leonardo da Vinci

Our Stories

My journey as a connected learner has occurred in just more than one-tenth of my life. I've now collaborated with people in my tomorrow. I've Skyped at 7 p.m. my local time while John in Australia was drinking his morning orange juice. With time and distance blurred, I've commiserated with colleagues in the far Southwest about the constraints imposed by high-stakes testing and brainstormed strategies to work around, in, and outside the system. I've participated in online sessions with experts, authors, and teachers as we sought to understand more fully how to influence the educational policies that affect our children's futures. In online communities, I've developed significant collegial relationships that I cherish; the opportunities to engage in difficult discussions around practice have kept me from sleep. Through networks on Twitter and in blogs, I've explored resources (ones I likely would never have discovered on my own) that have profoundly affected my beliefs about teaching and learning.

My journey into connected learning has been compelling, sometimes daunting, often exhilarating, yet always fueled by passion. I've embraced the exponential potential that connectedness has to transform learning. I've learned far more in my time as a connected learner than in those many years before. I welcome a future that I can't imagine and the opportunities it brings to continue my learning trek.

—Lani

Many web users, including educators, still think about the web primarily as a digital filing cabinet, a place where information resides and a place to search for resources, even though there is ample evidence it has evolved. (Think of the role social media played in the Arabic rebellions, for example.)

Connected learners know that the web is a place to find people, to exchange ideas, to share our imaginations, insights, and opinions. The web has become not only a great *curriculum* resource but also a great *learning* resource. And, if we so choose, each of us can add to the world's understanding and can advocate for positive change.

New technologies that make it easy to connect and collaborate online are challenging the traditional structures of many institutions, including schools. What happens to traditional concepts of classrooms, teaching and, most importantly, learning when any of us can learn anything, anywhere, at any time?

Neil Postman (1992) suggests, "A new technology does not add or subtract something. It changes everything" (p. 18). If Postman is right, learning has to be affected when we use different methods and cognitive structures to process information. As technologies evolve and classroom learning strategies change in response, 21st century learning will not be just a variation of the past. Even now, connected learners gain knowledge in ways very different from how our parents and grandparents went about learning.

Are Teachers Relevant Without Change?

Psychologist and computer scientist Roger Schank has developed a theory of cognitive learning. Schank's Law states:

> Because people understand by finding in their memories the closest possible match to what they are hearing and use that match as the basis of comprehension, any new idea will be treated as a variant of something the listener has already thought of or heard. Agreement with a new idea means a listener has already had a similar thought and well appreciates that the speaker has recognized his idea. Disagreement means the opposite. Really new ideas are incomprehensible. The good news is that for some people, failure to comprehend is the beginning of understanding. For most, of course, it is the beginning of dismissal. (Schank, 2004)

As Schank says, learning is about making schematic connections, attaching new knowledge to existing understandings. Piaget refers to learning as moving from a state of disequilibrium to one of assimilation of new ideas (Piaget, 1962; Piaget & Inhelder, 1969). Learning is a jumping-off place where we not only attach new ideas to the old and assimilate them but make peace with the fact that we have to unlearn much of the knowledge we started with.

By developing an adaptive mindset, the connected learner can innovate. Because technologies connect us and the potential now is to create a generation of participatory curriculum designers (you and your students), innovation is multiplied rather than added. The shift is exponential rather than incremental. Schools will change or become irrelevant. Teachers will redefine themselves and their classrooms, or students will turn elsewhere in order to learn.

Think About

Does your district have opportunities for policy changes that would support connected learning? Could an action research project examine the possibility and pilot implementation of such a policy shift?

Learning 2.0: Four Core Components

As you start to think about change in technology and education, do not change *anything* about how you teach or lead. Instead, change *everything* about how you learn. Be selfish for a time, and make everything about you and your learning. By becoming a *learner first and educator second*, you are serving your students and will be in a better position to model lifelong adaptive learning strategies for your students. You can't give what you do not own. Play, explore, connect, ask questions, think deeply, reflect, and collaborate within your personal learning network, community of practice, and professional learning community—your connected learning communities. Figure out what change means for you in the four core components of Learning 2.0—knowledge, pedagogy, connections, and capacity.

Knowledge

With information increasing at its current rate, no one will be able to master all the knowledge in any discipline. Our job is to nurture the collective intelligence of our classrooms and to build collective intelligence through our connected learning communities. Remember, it isn't so much about what you know or what your students can memorize. Rather, it is about an awareness of your network's expertise and knowing how to connect your students to that wisdom.

Pedagogy

A connected learner's vision of teaching moves from "I am the teacher" to helping students chase their passions, empowering them to find their voices online and off, creating classrooms free from threat and stress, and forming a school environment that not only extends beyond the classroom walls but encourages risk taking, creativity, and innovation. The questions become, What is the best pedagogy for real-world learning experiences? How does that shift when teachers use technology to connect, collaborate, and co-construct? How does the relationship between content, technology, and pedagogy change when used to support passion-based learning?

Connections

Learning 2.0 means modeling for students (and in some cases them modeling for us) how to create sustained personal learning networks where we experiment and share with online colleagues, connect to content experts, and use technology for scholarship. Connected educators become experts in creating knowledge in networks (connectivism), and leveraging that knowledge, to inform student learning. Connected educators also understand how to move beyond networks into global communities in which the members think and act deeply as they seek to improve practice.

Capacity

Capacity building has been described as "an ongoing process through which individuals, groups, organizations and societies enhance their ability to identify and meet development challenges" (Catholic Relief Services, 2011). Relationships are the currency of capacity building. Connected learning communities allow individuals and groups to build capacity and students and educators to build self- and collective efficacy.

Putting the learner first is a different way of thinking. Rather than preconceived ideas of what learners (adults or children) should do, say, and produce, we adopt a mindset of discovery and remain open to what talents and interests we may find in each learner.

The Evolution of the Teacher

Connected leaders and learners shift from seeing education as a series of things we do *to* students and teachers and instead as dynamic learning environments in which learners take ownership of their own growth and pursue it passionately. The web and other powerful social technologies offer opportunities that we can integrate into the learning experience. But the shift is not primarily about changing the tools we use. It is about transforming the way most teachers teach today. They teach this way either because they were taught to teach in that manner or because the accountability system makes them believe they have to.

When we shift to a new way of teaching and learning, assessment becomes a proactive process embedded in learning and designed to help the learner understand how to improve and learn more. The shift in teaching and learning requires more from teachers than just throwing out a few clarifying questions. When learning rules the school structure, teachers will have evolved beyond delivering curriculum—beyond simply deconstructing knowledge into bite-sized pieces for students to memorize and regurgitate on tests. Instead, they will be connected coaches who understand how to use appreciative inquiry to help students construct and validate their own learning.

Questions for the Change Agent in You

A change agent is someone who intentionally or indirectly causes or accelerates social, cultural, or behavioral change. You have the ability to cause positive change in your school and be an educational activist. Such an attitude means rethinking your perspectives and asking yourself tough questions, such as, "Am I the box?" The following questions, inspired and adapted with permission from Bill Taylor (2009), will help you deepen your thinking about your role.

1. **Do you see opportunities for positive change that others at your school do not see?** French novelist Marcel Proust famously said, "The real act of discovery consists not in finding new lands but in seeing with new eyes." The most successful change agents don't do *more* . . . they do *differently*. They redefine the terms of education by embracing one-of-a-kind ideas.

2. **Do you have new ideas about where to look for new ideas?** One way to look at problems as if you're seeing them for the first time is to look outside of education. Look for ideas that have worked in other fields. Ideas that are routine in one area can be revolutionary when they migrate to another, especially when they challenge the prevailing assumptions that have come to define school culture.

3. **Are your ideas really good?** Your ideas for educational reform cannot be pretty good; they need to be really good. They need to be the most of something: the most affordable, the most accessible, the most elegant, the most colorful, the most transparent, the most *kids*.

4. **If your idea or mission didn't happen, who would miss you and why?** Jim Collins, author of *Good to Great*, talks about this. The question is simple and worth taking seriously as a guide to what really matters. *As a change agent, do you add value or just create noise?*

5. **Have you figured out how your school's history can help shape its future?** Psychologist Jerome Bruner (1983) describes what happens when we use what works to define what is new. The essence of creativity, he argues, is "figuring out how to use what you already know in order to go beyond what you already think" (p. 183). The most creative leaders don't disavow the past. They rediscover and reinterpret what has come before as a way to develop a line of sight into what comes next.

6. **Are you getting the best contributions from the most people?** Change is not a game best played by loners. These days the most powerful contributions come from the most unexpected places—the hidden genius inside your personal learning network, the collective genius of other smart people who surround you. Do you know how to tap into genius?

continued →

7. **Are you consistent in your commitment to change?** Schools often are accused of not having the courage to change. In fact, the problem with many schools is that all they do is change. They lurch from one unfounded idea to the next, from the most recent instructional fad to the newest technology craze. If, as a change agent, you want to make deep-seated change, then your priorities and practices have to remain consistent in good times and bad. Action research can help you target what works and guide you in developing a long-term plan for positive change.

8. **Are you learning as quickly as the world is changing?** In a world that never stops changing, great leaders never stop learning. How do you push yourself as an individual to keep growing and evolving so that your school can do the same?

Although we have done this work, we are continuing to learn. Like all restless lifelong learners, we have more questions than answers. Here are some of the things we think about.

- What principled changes should *we* be making in our classrooms to ensure that we are developing in students the skill sets they will need as they face future challenges?

- Are we preparing kids for yesterday, today, or tomorrow?

- Are current classroom techniques helping those we teach become future scientists, technologists, and imagineers who will solve the social ills of the society of the future?

- How can we collectively advocate best for needed policy changes that will enable our teachers and students to engage in connected, authentic learning?

- How can we help our students be ready to learn using tools we cannot yet imagine?

As you think about how to become a connected learner or continue on your journey, revisit these questions and develop your own answers, or add to the questions to advance your learning. To paraphrase Gandhi, be the change you want to see in the world.

Our Charge to You

Newton's first Law of Motion, the Law of Inertia, applies to you, too: "An object at rest tends to stay at rest, and an object in motion tends to stay in motion with the same speed and in the same direction unless acted upon by an unbalanced force" (Newton's Laws of Motion, 2011).

What will change because you read and connected through this book? Have we served as that *unbalanced force*? We hope so.

We understand that this is a tough time to be an educator. Many report feeling helpless about making change in their classrooms and schools due to _____ (testing pressure, budget cuts, lack of technology, lack of support, lack of time—you fill in the blank). And while each excuse may have some validity, the truth is that they are just that—excuses.

Change is not easy. Teaching to multiple-choice tests is easy. It's easy to try out a few web tools and put a check in the box next to *change agent*. Turning your classroom or school into a place where deep learning occurs and learners' needs are being met is *hard*. Educational change is hard because it involves re-culturing—re-examining values and dispositions and letting go of what we are vested in.

Teaching is, at its core, a moral profession. Helping students become connected, passion-driven learners is a moral issue. Most of us went into education to change the world, to help kids, to make a difference, and somewhere along the way, many of us lost sight of that moral purpose.

We all have a choice: A choice to be powerful or pitiful. A choice to allow ourselves to become victims or activists. A choice to take a stand on behalf of the children we serve.

The world is at your fingertips. Figure out your personal vision for change in your school or classroom. Learn how to leverage the wisdom of the crowd. Build alliances. Find your tribe, your community. Then do something powerful to promote change. Sit down with other educators and share what you learn. Be a transparent learner. Be the example you want your students to become. Show them what a learner does to make the world a better place.

Choose to be powerful.

Glossary

asynchronous learning. Learning that is not *live* or dependent on the learner being in a certain place at a certain time. Asynchronous learning is flexible, allowing people choices about when to participate. Some examples are discussion forums, social network settings (such as Ning communities), email distribution lists, self-paced courses, and archived webinars.

blog. Short for *weblog*, a blog is a website that is continually updated with journal-like entries called *posts*, which are usually arranged in chronological order with the most recent post appearing first. Many blogs include a link at the end of a post for readers to use to add comments.

Bloglines. An RSS (Really Simple Syndication) feed aggregator.

cloud computing. Internet-based computing in which the software, content, and storage capacity a user needs reside on remote servers (the *cloud*), rather than on the user's device (personal computer, tablet, or mobile phone). The needed resources are provided to computers and other devices on demand, like electricity.

collaboration and collaborative learning. Joint intellectual efforts, such as when learners work together in a classroom or course to find meaning or to create an artifact of their learning.

collegiality. Believing that none of us is as good as all of us, or even that none of us is as smart as all of us together; believing that the contributions of all can lead to improved individual practice.

communities of inquiry (CoI). Groups that collaborate and engage in questioning and problem solving in order to develop a shared understanding; members engage in authentic inquiry.

communities of practice (CoP). Communities made up of local and global members; these communities are characterized as systems of collective critical inquiry and reflection focused on building a shared identity.

congenial. When individuals are interactive, positive, friendly, and personal in their interactions with one another.

connected learning communities (CLCs). Groups that connect and collaborate in local communities (professional learning communities), global networks (personal learning networks), and bounded global communities (communities of practice), leveraging and bridging knowledge and expertise across these networks and communities to grow and continually improve professional practice.

connectivism. A model of learning that acknowledges the tremendous shifts in learning afforded by current technologies in a rapidly changing sea of information.

cooperative. A style of working together in which each member of a group performs a unique role to accomplish a common task.

Creative Commons. These licenses allow creators to communicate which rights they reserve and which rights they waive for the benefit of recipients or other creators. An easy-to-understand, one-page explanation of rights, with associated visual symbols, explains the specifics of each Creative Commons license. This simplicity distinguishes Creative Commons from an all-rights-reserved copyright.

crowdsourcing. The act of outsourcing tasks through an open call. For example, the public may be invited to develop a new technology, carry out a design task, or contribute ideas.

dashboard. A screen with floating windows used to administrate a website. For example, a dashboard for blogging software might have an RSS feed of news about the blogging software, a space to write a new post, an area to approve comments, and a place to administrate users for the blog.

Delicious. A web-based social bookmarking tool.

Diigo. A web-based social bookmarking tool.

direct message. Also called a DM, these are private tweets between the sender and the recipient.

DIY. Abbreviation for *do-it-yourself.*

Edublogs. Free blogs for teachers.

Elgg. Open-source social networking software that offers blogging, microblogging, file sharing, networking, groups, and a number of other features.

Elluminate. A software application with virtual rooms, or vSpaces, where virtual schools and businesses can hold classes and meetings.

Facebook. A social networking service with more than six hundred million users.

Facebook group. A way of enabling a number of people to come together online via Facebook to share information and discuss specific subjects.

Flickr. A web-based photo sharing site with social networking elements.

Google Docs. A web-based document sharing tool that takes the place of software such as Microsoft Office for generating word-processing documents and spreadsheets.

Google Reader. An RSS (Really Simple Syndication) feed aggregator.

hashtag. A word on Twitter beginning with the # symbol, used to mark keywords or topics in a Tweet. It can be used to track topics or to search for a keyword.

HootSuite. A Twitter application that acts as a dashboard for all of a user's Twitter activity through a setup of vertical columns users can customize.

inquiry. A student-centered approach to learning in which students learn by questioning.

International Society for Technology in Education (ISTE). A not-for-profit organization that supports the use of information technology to aid learning and teaching in grades K–12.

International Society for Technology in Education National Educational Technology Standards (ISTE NETS). Broad goals for connected educators, both administrators and teachers, to develop national standards for educational uses of technology.

K12Online Conference. The first free, educator-led, totally online conference, co-founded by Sheryl Nussbaum-Beach.

LISTSERV™. An electronic mailing list consisting of a set of email addresses for a group. A listserv allows the sender to email an entire group simultaneously.

messy conversation. An open and honest conversation in which difficult or uncomfortable questions may be raised, but both parties walk away having learned something from the other.

microblogging. Using tools such as Twitter or Plurk, users create microblog entries of less than 140 characters.

Moodle. A free, open-source e-learning software platform.

National Council of Teachers of English (NCTE). A professional association of educators in English, literacy, and language arts.

Netvibes. A dashboard service that allows users to view real-time web updates all on one page on the content they find useful.

Ning. An online platform that allows people to create their own social networks around a topic, interest, or group.

node. Any element that can be connected to any other element.

personal learning network (PLN). A network composed of personal online and offline connections with others who are globally situated and who share a common passion for sharing ideas and resources, both professional and personal.

PLPeep. A participant in the Powerful Learning Practice experience.

podcasts. Postings similar to blogs but that are audio or video files. Users can subscribe using RSS technology and receive a notification each time a new audio or video file is published.

Podomatic. A free tool to help users record, produce, and publish podcasts to the web.

Powerful Learning Practice (PLP). A professional development company founded by Sheryl Nussbaum-Beach and Will Richardson that helps job-embedded teams of educators learn to manage change in networks and communities.

professional learning communities (PLCs). Local communities of educators who work and learn together face-to-face to increase their professional knowledge and enhance student learning and achievement.

professional learning team (PLT). A team made up of Powerful Learning Practice (PLP) community members who share knowledge and collaborate on action research.

re-culturing. Changing the beliefs, norms, and values of a community.

remix. An alternative or nonlinear reinterpretation of any media, such as a song, video, or piece of literature.

reputation management. The practice of monitoring a user's Internet reputation by proactively creating a positive web presence for oneself. This includes filling out Google profiles or bio pages on blogs and community portals, being a present and contributing member in social networks, being visible online so that one's name appears in listings when typed into Google, and suppressing negative mentions by attempting to push them lower in search engine results.

retweet. Another user's tweet (Twitter message) that someone you follow forwards you. Often used to spread news or share valuable findings on Twitter. Users can retweet another user's tweets to share the message with their own followers.

RSS (Really Simple Syndication). A family of news feed formats that are used to publish updated work (podcasts, blogs, and videos). Readers can subscribe to a feed and aggregate a number of feeds in a reader.

Skype. A software application that allows users to make voice calls over the Internet.

social bookmarking. A web-based application that lets users organize links by keywords or tags and then share their bookmarks with other users on the site and around the web.

social media. Web-based and mobile technologies that users turn to for communication and interactive dialogue.

social network. A social structure made up of individuals (or organizations) called nodes that are connected in one or more ways, such as through friendship, kinship, common interest, and financial exchange.

synchronous learning. People learning at the same time; *live* learning. On the Internet, typical examples include webinars and activities in conferencing environments, such as Elluminate or GoToMeeting, or simply via audio and instant chat using a tool like Skype.

tag. A keyword used to describe the content being organized for easier retrieval.

tagging. Also known as social bookmarking or folksonomy. A way of organizing websites, photos, videos, blog posts, or other content accessed online by grouping similar items together under labels.

TeacherTube. An online community for sharing educational videos made for teachers by teachers.

three-pronged approach. A model of connected learning proposed by Powerful Learning Practice in which individuals engage in three kinds of learning environments: (1) professional learning communities, (2) personal learning networks, and (3) communities of practice. (See separate glossary entries for those terms.)

TweetDeck. Twitter application that acts as a dashboard for all of a user's Twitter activity with a setup of vertical columns that can be customized for individual preferences.

Twitter. A web-based microblogging platform; an information network of 140-character messages from users all over the world.

Twitter lists. Curated groups of other Twitter users, used to tie specific individuals into a group on a user's Twitter account.

Twitterverse. All Twitter users; the Twitter universe.

URL address. Uniform Resource Locator, an address denoting the location of a website, for example, www.google.com.

VoiceThread. An online application that allows users to have a collaborative conversation. The VoiceThread can consist of images, video clips, sound recordings, and more. (http://voicethread.com)

Wallwisher. A web-based application that functions as a collaborative virtual notice board, allowing users to post virtual sticky notes including images, text, video, and links. (http://wallwisher.com)

Web 2.0. A term for web applications that facilitate participatory information sharing, interoperability, user-centered design, and collaboration on the web.

walled garden. A private or closed online social networking community.

widget. A small representation of an application that you put on a webpage for specific information or functionality, similar to apps for smartphones.

Wikipedia. An online, wiki-based encyclopedia that is user-generated and operates without an editorial staff.

wiki. A webpage that groups of people can edit together. That is, anyone can change what appears on the page.

Wikispaces. A tool to facilitate creating and managing a wiki.

YouTube. A web-based video-sharing tool with social networking components.

Research Base for the Connected Learning Community Model

A vast body of literature underlies the connected learning communities model. Here we cite the studies and literature most relevant to connected learning in the digital age and supporting points to help readers understand the rationale behind connected learning. We've grouped the findings by the three components of connected learning communities: professional learning communities (PLCs), personal learning networks (PLNs), and communities of practice (CoPs). After a brief description of each component's characteristics, we delve into its underlying theories, experience and knowledge, effectiveness for teacher professional development, anticipated growth or decline, challenges and dilemmas, and use of technology.

Visit http://diigo.com/tag/clcresearch (tag: clcresearch) to deepen your knowledge of these studies.

Professional Learning Communities

The literature proposes the characteristics of professional learning communities in which educators are connected and engage in face-to-face collaboration: collaborative learning with a purposeful shared vision and practice and a focus on inquiry and improvement building (Hord, 1997). Kruse, Louis, and Bryk (1995), Little (1993), and McLaughlin and Talbert (2001) concur with Hord's findings and suggest that professional learning community members engage in reflective conversations and exhibit mutual support for each other, while DuFour (2004) suggests that professional learning communities focus on learning and result in a culture of collaboration with the clear purpose of affecting professional practice and improving student achievement.

These characteristics found in the literature—collaborative learning, shared vision, reflective conversations, a focus on inquiry, and improved student learning—clearly align with dispositions of connected learning.

Theories

The literature notes a number of theories relevant to professional learning communities; the underlying assumptions of each of these theories play a prominent role in the self-directed 21st century learning of a connected educator. The social nature of learning is found throughout (Bandura, 1977; Wenger, 2006); adult learning theory is also evident. Galluci (2007) alludes to Vygotskian theory as she examines the shift from private to publicly shared learning. Wood (2007) identifies a "Deweyan approach" when educators participate in collaborative, inquiry-based discussions. Theories of situated learning in *communities of practice*, in which learning and practice go hand-in-hand in a social environment where discussions of practice among experts are indispensable to novice practitioners (Lave & Wenger, 1991), are woven throughout the literature. In addition, Schmoker (2004) and the Annenberg Institute for School Reform (2004) recognize an alignment with adult development theory that is found in the self-directed, job-embedded problem solving that occurs in professional learning communities.

These underlying theories, which posit social learning, collaborative inquiry, and a movement from private to public, are a basic piece of the foundation of connected learning.

Experience and Knowledge

The literature indicates members of professional learning communities focus on relationships around learning (Stoll, Bolam, McMahon, Wallace, & Thomas, 2006), relationships comparable to those needed for and found in 21st century connected learning. Annenberg Institute for School Reform (2004) notes a commitment to improve practice and knowledge of content, while DuFour (2004) concludes that members are committed to improvement where perseverance is important. The National School Reform Faculty (2008) found openness, trust, and supportive leadership to be important when working with critical friends' groups in learning communities. Wood (2007) notes the ability to manage conflict and build consensus are needed skills.

The critical place of collegial relationships in connected learning is well supported in the literature, as is the need for trust and openness. Educators who value the experience and knowledge brought to professional learning communities have begun to travel the path of connected learning.

Effectiveness for Teacher Professional Development

Are professional learning communities a viable means to improve teacher learning? Determining professional learning communities' effectiveness is a challenge given their collaborative structure and broad goals and that the literature around this topic often uses descriptive case studies of individual groups. Yet indications are that the connected, collaborative learning characteristics of professional learning communities do result in positive shifts in educator learning. Fullan (2006) proposes that how a professional learning community impacts improvement in a particular school or district may be a meaningful measure of effectiveness. In a review of eleven studies, Vescio, Ross, and Adams (2008) find that the teaching culture and collaboration improved as teachers focused more on student learning. Guldberg and Pilkington (2006), in a study of an online professional learning community, identify the potential for members of a networked learning opportunity to move from basic sharing to thoughtful, meaningful conversations that result in consensus on the qualities of best practice. Their findings hold promise for digital connected learning communities.

These findings—in particular that of networked learning moving educators from sharing to conversations around practice—provide additional validation for the premise that real change can occur from connecting and from the collaboration resulting from collegial relationships.

Anticipated Growth or Decline

The literature suggests growth in the use of professional learning communities to support teachers. Schmoker (2004) notes an increasing number of educators and researchers promoting the type of collaboration found in professional learning communities. Moreover, professional organizations indicate interest in professional learning communities, according to DuFour (2007). Both Fullan (2006) and Richardson (2005) note increased interest among teachers, and district websites also corroborate that interest.

With the increased interest in and growth of professional learning communities, the opportunities for extended collaborations in connected learning communities grow as well. As educators leverage the learning of other professional learning communities across networks and connected learning communities, the potential grows for systemic change in education.

Challenges and Dilemmas

Having challenges is a given. Various studies posit a variety of challenges and dilemmas that professional learning communities face, including demands for time (Hollins, McIntyre, DeBose, Hollins, & Towner, 2004) and the impact of school size; large schools often have a more difficult time developing a schoolwide sense of community (Stoll et al., 2006). In addition, improvement is more challenging in secondary schools (Wells & Feun, 2007). Finally, the location of a school in a rural or isolated area, the climate of the student body, and the school's history can affect the effectiveness of a learning community (Hollins et al., 2004), as well as issues arising from people unfamiliar with working together needing to engage in difficult conversations (Stoll et al., 2006; Wells & Feun, 2007).

Realizing those challenges of time, of developing a sense of community, and of developing collegial relationships that preclude educators working together, we've explored each of these topics in various chapters. With supportive distributed leadership, these challenges and others can be met and overcome and the work of professional learning communities is one step closer toward becoming the change we want to see.

Use of Technology

A number of studies note the opportunities today's technologies provide to facilitate the connection of expertise among members and to allow for interaction (Dalgarno & Colgan, 2007; Lieberman, 2000; MacIsaac, 2000). Lieberman (2000) sees the online venue as ideal for connecting and collaborating in the quest for an improved practice, while MacIsaac (2000) notes the potential of these venues for unleashing the boundaries of space and time. Smith (2003) notes that technology encourages those who have not been self-directed, independent learners. Finally, Jeppesen and Frederiksen (2006) find that educators who embrace collaboration in online environments are often innovators and risk takers and consequently can become significant contributors as community members learn together.

We see technology as the amplifier and enabler of connected learning. Not only does technology, in one way, address the challenge of time by creating opportunities for connecting, collaborating, and reflecting 24/7 anywhere, but the literature findings also support the call for learners who collaborate, self-direct, and seek to continually develop expertise.

Personal Learning Networks

Although the body of literature on personal learning networks may not be as expansive as that on professional learning communities, numerous studies note the openness, connectedness, and personalized characteristics of personal learning networks. Personal learning networks are just that—personal (Johnson, Levine, & Smith, 2009)—and as such are composed of various connections including blogs, images, audio, and people (Downes, 2006) that provide learners with links to the world (Illich, 1970). With their open content (Downes, 2007b), personal learning networks are decentralized, distributed, democratized, and dynamic (Downes, 2006) as learners select resources about their own interests, seek out diverse voices (Berge & McElvaney, 2009) to deepen learning, and are free to turn to other areas of interest. Characterized by sharing (Downes, 2009; Grosseck & Holotescu, 2009; Ivanova, 2009) and reciprocity, personal learning networks are one component in the shift from an individual understanding to an understanding that is more systemic (Borgatti & Foster, 2003). Learners grow their personal learning networks in public spaces where people gather through mediating technology (boyd, 2007); these spaces share properties of persistence, searchability, and replicability (boyd, 2007). Consequently, learners can replicate, to the extent they desire, the characteristics of other's personal learning networks, and because of the mediating technology, learners can search and locate resources and ideas that have been posted in public. Often personal learning networks are seen as ways of organizing connections (Siemens, 2003). Similar to change adoption and technology adoption, personal learning networks' growth and use may be characterized by stages, which Utecht (2008) identifies as immersion, evaluation, know-it-all, perspective, and balance.

Connected learners leverage the potential for personalized learning through the diverse connections they seek and select for their learning. As they develop personal learning networks, they can bring the ideas from across networks into communities where they then dig deeper.

Theories

In contrast to professional learning communities, the literature on personal learning networks clearly points to connectivism and learner-centered approaches as the underlying theories. Siemens views learning as creating a network of connections and finding patterns (Siemens, 2005b, 2006, 2008), which supports the path for learners in creating personal learning networks—connections with people, resources, and objects. In addition, Darken and Sibert (1996) view personal learning networks through the lens of a learner who uses cues to achieve mastery.

The paradigm for sense making for many connected educators is connectivism. In our connected learning model, a network of personalized connections is an essential component that broadens learning potential.

Experience and Knowledge

Research suggests the knowledge educators bring to personal learning networks is distributed across the network and found in the connections (Downes, 2006; Siemens, 2005a, 2005b).

In contrast to the knowledge brought to professional learning communities around relationships and the ability to come to consensus, educators bring to personal learning networks the knowledge from the connections that may be diverse and with which educators may disagree. Learners, as indicated in the connected learning dispositions, acquire the knowledge needed to participate meaningfully in both the network and community.

Effectiveness for Teacher Professional Development

Personal learning networks are viewed as an effective venue for sharing globally and for facilitating teacher learning as they enable access to content, experts, and global connections with fellow learners (Siemens, 2008). Personal learning networks also play a vital part in managing environments of complex information (Wright, 2007), which aptly describes our society faced with an overabundance of information. Knowledge creation, evaluation, and sharing occur in interactions in networks (Ivanova, 2009) as they enhance lifelong learning (Siemens, 2003). Lastly, it has been noted that successful networks for learners have been developed around readings, links, blog posts, images, user-created lessons, and others' reactions and feedback (Grosseck & Holotescu, 2009).

Our connected learning model, which this literature supports, clearly views personal learning networks as one of three prongs for teacher learning. Managing information in complex environments and sharing are important skills for educators that can be acquired through the building of and participation in personal learning networks.

Anticipated Growth or Decline

Interest in and growth of personal learning networks has been noted as educators contend with enormous technology shifts. Siemens (2008) notes significant growth in interest in and research on networks and also suggests that there is a growing dependence on networks to deal with complex changes in society (Siemens, 2008). As they believe there is always need for educators to update skills, Lewis and Romiszowski (1996) predict continued growth in personal learning networks.

As with professional learning communities, personal learning networks are in a growth phase. Hence, the time is right to seize the opportunity to adapt the concept of CLCs and enhance the potential for shifts in practice as educators learn and grow across both networks and communities.

Challenges and Dilemmas

While there are immense opportunities for learning from diverse sources, educators do face challenges of time (Utecht, 2008), a willingness to become more transparent and the vulnerability that accompanies that (Harris, 2007), and the need for developing literacies required for growing and creating good networks (Jenkins, 2006). In addition, educators face a possible learning curve in creating environments that enable the connections (Siemens, 2003) and as they learn to effectively use Twitter (King, 2009).

We recognize those challenges and take time to suggest solutions in this book as we explore developing a personal learning network in chapter 6, using Twitter in chapter 5, the issue of transparency in chapters 2 and 3, and time as an issue in chapter 6. As real as these challenges are, we contend that we cannot use them as excuses but rather collectively seek solutions in order to create the schools our children deserve.

Use of Technology

Although personal learning networks are not new, their potential has expanded exponentially with the affordances of current technology. There has been a significant growth of networked technologies for learning—both formal and informal (Siemens, 2008), technologies that create the means for dynamic interaction (Siemens, 2003). These technologies enable the finding, synthesizing, and evaluating of information (Conole, de Laat, Dillon, & Darby, 2006) and, in addition, allow for personalization (Berge & McElvaney, 2009).

Consequently, current learning networks, constructed by connected learners, have the capacity to be very personal. Connected educators can more easily locate meaningful connections as technology again amplifies the possibilities for learning.

Communities of Practice

Etienne Wenger is considered to be a leader in the field. In his and others' writings about communities of practice, deep collaboration around practice is a central characteristic. Members of communities of practice share a common concern for what it is they do (Wenger, 1998). With that common concern, members interact and share stories of practice (Iverson & McPhee, 2002) with the goal of improving practice by collaboratively constructing knowledge (Wenger, 1998). They are distinguished by their deep level of collaboration (Stuckey, 2001). Within the common culture of a community of practice is an interdependent system (Barab & Duffy, 2000) in which the diverse membership from novice to expert gives life to the community (Lave & Wenger, 1991). Communities of practice grow from existing networks (Wenger et al., 2002) and, similar to personal learning networks, have recognized life cycles including emerging, maturing, active, and dispersing (Barab, MaKinster, & Scheckler, 2003; Preece, 2000; Wenger, 1998; Wenger et al., 2002). Despite dispersing, the community's co-constructed knowledge becomes a part of practice.

Communities do come out of networks, and we contend that participation in communities characterized by deep collaboration can help educators collectively improve practice and learning for all students.

Theories

The literature identifies a number of theories underlying communities of practice. First, Lave and Wenger (1991) and McLaughlin (2003) note that theories of situated learning are found in communities of practice where learning and practice go hand-in-hand in a social environment and where discussions of practice among experts are indispensable to novice practitioners. Cognitive apprenticeship theory, which proposes professional learning in authentic workplace environments

(Collins, Brown, & Newman, 1989) and collaborative learning between novice and expert, is evident. Research also suggests that communities of practice are based on a social view of learning (Barab et al., 2003; Wenger, 1998) as well as situated cognition theory (Lave, 1991).

Connected learning communities align with and are grounded in these theories as we see educators of diverse skills and ideas collaborating to learn more about and improve practice.

Experience and Knowledge

In communities of practice, diverse members bring and share understandings of both tacit and explicit knowledge (Preece, 2004) and through social relationships view learning as process of changing practice (Brosnan & Burgess, 2003). Knowledge is found in individuals and in community (Wasko & Faraj, 2000). Consequently, Sharratt and Usoro (2003) view communities of practice as enablers and enhancers of knowledge development, and Wenger and Snyder (2000) note that knowledge development is found in communities of practice.

The research supports the need for participation in communities where educators co-create knowledge around practice and leverage networked learning to create systemic change.

Effectiveness for Teacher Professional Development

Although some evidence suggesting the effectiveness of communities of practice for teacher learning is anecdotal (Lai, Pratt, Anderson, & Stigter, 2006), Chris Dede, from Harvard's School of Education, notes that the pedagogical approach underlying more than half of teacher professional development is grounded in the communities of practice theory (Dede, Breit, Ketelhut, McCloskey, & Whitehouse, 2005). Other research finds that communities of practice have significant potential to improve teaching and learning (Sherer, Shea, & Kristensen, 2003) and that participation in communities of practice benefits both students and teachers (Riel & Fulton, 2001). Not only do communities of practice encourage collaboration and knowledge construction (Ardichvili, Page, & Wentling, 2002; Buysse, Sparkman, & Wesley, 2003), they also have significant potential for improving teaching and learning (Sherer et al., 2003).

From work in online communities of practice and this literature, we have learned that educator membership and participation in such communities enable powerful teacher learning that translates to improved learning for students. In these communities, because of the relationships that have developed, the real work of improving practice occurs—the deep collaboration and the messy work of engaging in difficult conversations.

Anticipated Growth or Decline

The literature indicates that online communities of practice are increasing rapidly (Baran & Çağıltay, 2006). Wenger (2006) asserts that a growing number of organizations are seeking to improve practice through communities of practice. In 2010, the U.S. Department of Education Office of Educational Technology began an initiative focused on online communities of practice in response to the newly adopted National Educational Technology Plan vision of teacher professional development (U.S. Department of Education, 2011). In addition, when communities of practice emerge from or leverage face-to face-interactions, they are likely to grow (Nichani & Hung, 2002).

The time is right. Communities of practice are in a growth phase. The literature supports the three-pronged approach in suggesting that participation in communities of practice can be leveraged across and between professional learning communities, which are local in nature and meet face-to-face. In fact, our Powerful Learning Practice model works with locally situated teams of educators who come together in an online community of practice.

Challenges and Dilemmas

Like professional learning communities and personal learning networks, communities of practice have challenges. Optimizing the design of an online community of practice to promote sociability and support membership (Schlager & Fusco, 2004) is critical to its success. In addition, community structures need to be established that motivate participation (Schwen & Hara, 2003), and communities of practice must constantly be cultivated (Kling & Courtright, 2003; Nichani & Hung, 2002). Maintaining a healthy community requires balancing change and stability (Stuckey & Smith, 2004). Finally, some communities disagree on expert practice (Palincsar, Magnusson, Marano, Ford, & Brown, 1998), hindering the community's vitality.

Use of Technology

As more communities of practice move to online spaces, using technology to support collaboration and knowledge building is crucial. As Riel and Fulton (2001) note, technology supports the community's interactions. In addition, technology needs to be designed for sociability (Cothrel & Williams, 1999; Davenport & Hall, 2002; Kling & Courtright, 2003; Schwen & Hara, 2003). Finally, effective networked technology supports the evolution of practice (Riel & Polin, 2004), influencing the coconstruction of knowledge.

These findings correlate with our experiences with online communities of practice. The significance of designing for sociability can't be overstated; those features that enhance sharing and co-creation of content impact the development of collegial relationships that are prerequisites to meaningful collaboration around improving practice. We are convinced that technology magnifies the potential for learning across communities, learning that when translated to practice will transform education for our students.

Appendix B

Scale in Action

Let's assume you have a proven educational innovation that you want to scale up. You may be wondering what *scale* is. *Scale* is the adaptation of your innovative project to almost any educational setting. But how do you take a really good idea and move it through the scale process? How do you make certain your innovation retains its quality while developing a larger reach? How do you ensure that, as it grows, it still results in improved educational outcomes for all students? The answer? Scale.

To help you think more deeply about scale, we have taken Powerful Learning Practice's model of connected learning communities through the five steps of scale: (1) depth, (2) sustainability, (3) spread, (4) shift, and (5) evolution. By giving you a concrete example of a project as it moves through the scale process, we hope you will become clearer about what you might need to do with your own innovations and projects.

A little background might help. Powerful Learning Practice was developed out of a collaborative project that Sheryl Nussbaum-Beach created with John Norton, an educational writer in North Carolina, and Cathy Gassenheimer, president of the Alabama Best Practices Center. The original model was to serve teachers across the state of Alabama who wanted to rethink their teaching practices as 21st century learners rather than 21st century teachers. It was funded by a Microsoft Partners in Learning grant. The work was so successful in Alabama that Sheryl approached Will Richardson about taking the model global, and together they cofounded Powerful Learning Practice.

Table B.1 (page 164) outlines the timeline of that process through the five dimensions of scale. As you examine the chart, think about your own project in each of these dimensions.

Table B.1: Illustrations of Scale From the 21st Century Learners Project to Powerful Learning Practice

Dimensions of Scale	Sources of Leverage for Scale	Alabama Best Practices Center: 21st Century Learner Model	Powerful Learning Practice
Depth Profound and lasting changes in practice	Engaging in research and evaluation to understand effectiveness	Microsoft required regular reflections based on dimensions of scale. For example, here is one lesson learned as it relates to depth: **Lesson**—Use your own research and evaluation to make changes that increase depth and quality. Envision your project, from the first day, as being on an evolutionary path. As your project matures, be prepared to rethink it based on your participants' behaviors and adaptations • We stayed abreast of current research around 21st century change. • Alabama Best Practices Center hired an external evaluator. • We did a content analysis of posts in a community of practice.	Built on research used to develop the 21st Century Learner model Used additional research on collaborative and connected learning, critical friends, action research, and coaching To understand effectiveness and learn deeply about how the model works, we: • Synthesized and interpreted ongoing survey data from participants • Carried out empirical research (content analysis of posts) in third year with Australian Netbooks project on knowledge construction • Reviewed and aggregated reflections from those using Powerful Learning Practice for graduate credit
Sustainability Maintaining profound changes over time	Creating a robust design to enable adapting to negative shifts in context	No longer dependent on Microsoft funding with support of state professional development network, school-based funding, and Alabama Best Practices Center administrative support	Based on need, tapped into school or district professional development funding Adapted costs of participation to numbers and years commitment Changed design based on feedback to make it more robust For example, allowed virtual participants and smaller teams, and expanded what we offered, that is, e-courses and virtual institutes

Dimensions of Scale	Sources of Leverage for Scale	Alabama Best Practices Center: 21st Century Learner Model	Powerful Learning Practice
Spread Entrenching the initiative's norms and principles with the organization and increasing participation (numbers of educators)	Adapting to maintain integrity of the initiative despite changes in resources and expertise	**Year 1:** Twenty schools **Year 2:** Forty additional schools **Year 3:** Demonstration sites in ten schools Added face-to-face component in year two Added fellows to share work load in year two	**Year 1:** Four twenty-team cohorts with five-member teams **Year 2:** Ten twenty-team cohorts with five-member teams (with international team participation) with advanced learning for year-two teams who could participate with two-member teams; added three-day boot camp for administrators **Year 3:** Eleven twenty-team cohorts with five-member teams using advanced curriculum for years two and three participants, plus added a virtual institute option, and two administrative boot camps, as well as expanded reach to a full cohort in Australia **Year 4:** Thirteen twenty-team cohorts with five-member teams using advanced curriculum for year-two and year-three teams, continued virtual institute option, added a global cohort option with no face-to-face participation, and expanded administrative boot camps to Norway

continued →

Dimensions of Scale	Sources of Leverage for Scale	Alabama Best Practices Center: 21st Century Learner Model	Powerful Learning Practice
Shift Moving ownership from external to internal within the community or organization	Supporting internal participants as they grow ownership	Encouraged districts to adapt reform effort to meet their needs Talladega County (Alabama) Schools customized the model. Added projects that created the possibility for shift through an action plan Powerful Learning Practice was created as an adapted model.	Each professional learning team creates an action research project that extends concepts to member schools and districts. Many districts designed similar professional development opportunities for schools in their area. Hired a social networking team that promotes and celebrates efforts of teams to own and shift concepts to their own context Hired a consultant to create the blog Voices From the Learning Revolution, which further shifts ownership to Powerful Learning Practice participants
Evolution Adapting, revising, and consequently impacting the thoughts of the original designers	Rethinking the original innovation based on revisions and adaptations of other users	Incorporated the adaptations of Talladega County into the statewide model Model is now intertwined with all the work of the Alabama Best Practices Center.	Powerful Learning Practice has evolved over the course of three years, having been rethought based on adaptations of the model by users and their adaptations. Empirical study underway to look at all Powerful Learning Practice cohorts to learn more about user adaptations in an effort to evolve the model even more

Common Diigo and Twitter Hashtags

Here we've listed some tags you can use to find and add to the collective bookmarks on Diigo or to organize chats on Twitter.

#connectededc

Anything related to the book overall

#clc-voc

Glossary items and common language

#clcresearch

Research supporting the connected learning community model

#clc-tools

Web 2.0 tools for connected learners

#clc-community

Resources related to building community

#clc-network

Resources related to building networks

#clc-plp

Discussions about Powerful Learning Practice

References and Resources

Aceto, S., Dondi, C., & Marzotto, P. (2010). *Pedagogical innovation in new learning communities: An in-depth study of twelve online learning communities.* European Commission, Joint Research Centre, Institute for Prospective Technological Studies. Luxembourg: Publications Office of the European Union. Accessed at http://ftp.jrc.es/EURdoc/JRC59474.pdf on June 13, 2011.

Annenberg Institute for School Reform. (2004). *Professional learning communities: Professional development strategies that improve instruction.* Providence, RI: Author. Accessed at www.annenberginstitute.org/pdf/proflearning.pdf on June 13, 2011.

Apple, M. W., & Beane, J. A. (1999). *Democratic schools: Lessons from the chalk face.* Buckingham: Open University Press.

Ardichvili, A., Page, V., & Wentling, T. (2002, April). *Motivation and barriers to participation in virtual knowledge-sharing communities of practice.* Paper presented at the Third European Conference on Organizational Knowledge, Learning and Capabilities, Athens, Greece.

Atherton, J. S. (2011). Group development. *Teaching and learning.* Accessed at www.learningandteaching.info/teaching/group_development.htm on June 13, 2011.

Atkins, D. E., Bennett, J., Brown, J. S., Chopra, A., Dede, C., Fishman, B., et al. (2010). *Transforming American education: Learning powered by technology.* Washington, DC: U.S. Department of Education.

Bandura, A. (1977). *Social learning theory.* Englewood Cliffs, NJ: Prentice Hall.

Barab, S. A., & Duffy, T. M. (2000). From practice fields to communities of practice. In D. H. Jonassen & S. M. Land (Eds.), *Theoretical foundations of learning environments* (pp. 25–56). Mahwah, NJ: Erlbaum.

Barab, S. A., ILF Design Team, MaKinster, J. G., Moore, J. A., & Cunningham, D. J. (2001). Designing and building an online community: The struggle to support sociability in the inquiry learning forum. *Educational Technology Research and Development, 49*(4), 71–96.

Barab, S., MaKinster, J., & Moore, J. (2001). Designing and building an online community: The struggle to support sociability in the Inquiry Learning Forum. *Educational Technology Research and Development, 49*(4), 71–96.

Barab, S. A., MaKinster, J. G., & Scheckler, R. (2003). Designing system dualities: Characterizing a web-supported professional development community. *Information Society, 19*(3), 237–256.

Barab, S. A., Moore, J., Cunningham, D., & ILF Design Team. (2000). *The Internet learning forum: A new model for online professional development.* Accessed at http://inkido.indiana.edu/research/onlinemanu/papers/ilfdesign.pdf on June 14, 2011.

Baran, B., & Çağıltay, K. (2006). Knowledge management and online communities of practice in teacher education. *Turkish Online Journal of Educational Technology, 5*(3), 1303–6521.

Barth, R. (2000). The teacher leader: Words of wisdom from those who know best. *Edutopia.* Accessed at www.edutopia.org/teacher-leader on June 14, 2011.

Barth, R. S. (2001a). *Learning by heart.* San Francisco: Jossey-Bass.

Barth, R. S. (2001b). Teacher leader. *Phi Delta Kappan, 82*(6), 443–449.

Barth, R. S. (2006). Improving relationships within the schoolhouse. *Educational Leadership, 63*(6), 8–13. Accessed at www.allthingsplc.info/pdf/articles/improving relationships.pdf on June 14, 2011.

Baumeister, H-P. (2005). Networked learning in the knowledge economy: A systemic challenge for universities. *European Journal of Open, Distance, and E-Learning.* Accessed at www.eurodl.org/materials/contrib/2005/Baumeister.htm on January 10, 2008.

Beaumont, C. (2009, January 16). New York plane crash: Twitter breaks the news, again. *Telegraph.* Accessed at www.telegraph.co.uk/technology/twitter/4269765/New -York-plane-crash-Twitter-breaks-the-news-again.html on September 17, 2010.

Berry, B., & TeacherSolutions 2030 Team. (2011). *Teaching 2030: What we must do for our students and our public schools . . . now and in the future.* New York: Teachers College Press.

Bezzina, C., & Vidoni, D. (2006). *Nurturing learning communities: A guide to school-based professional development* (CRELL Research Paper 3). Luxembourg: Office for Official Publications of the European Communities. Accessed at http://crell.jrc .ec.europa.eu/publications/crell%20research%20papers/school%20leadership%20 eur.pdf on June 14, 2011.

Bielaczyc, K., & Collins, A. (1999). Learning communities in classrooms: A reconceptualization of educational practice. In C. M. Reigeluth (Ed.), *Instructional-design theories and models: A new paradigm of instructional theory* (Vol. 2, pp. 269–292). Mahwah, NJ: Erlbaum.

Block, P. (2008). *Community: The structure of belonging.* San Francisco: Berrett-Koehler.

Bolam, R., McMahon, A., Stoll, L., Thomas, S., & Wallace, M. (2005). *Creating and sustaining effective professional learning communities* [Research Report No. 637]. Nottingham, UK: University of Bristol Department for Education and Skills. Accessed at www.education.gov.uk/publications/eOrderingDownload/RR637 .pdf on June 14, 2011.

Borgatti, S. P., & Foster, P. C. (2003). The network paradigm in organizational research: A review and typology. *Journal of Management, 29*(6), 991–1013.

boyd, d. (2007). Social network sites: Public, private, or what? *The Knowledge Tree: An e-Journal of Learning Innovation.* Accessed at http://kt.flexiblelearning.net.au /tkt2007/edition-13/social-network-sites-public-private-or-what/ on June 15, 2011.

Bransford, J. D., Brown, A. L., & Cocking, R.R. (Eds.). (1999). *How people learn: Brain, mind, experience, and school.* Washington, DC: National Academy Press.

Bretag, R. (2007). The simple reality [Web log post]. *Metanoia.* Accessed at www.ryanbretag .com/blog/?p=222 on June 15, 2011.

Brosnan, K., & Burgess, R. C. (2003). Web based continuing professional development— A learning architecture approach. *Journal of Workplace Learning, 15*(1), 24–33.

Brown, J. S. (2001). Learning to unlearn. *Storytelling: Passport to the 21st century.* Accessed at www.creatingthe21stcentury.org/JSB3-learning-to-unlearn.html on June 15, 2011.

Bruner, J. S. (1983). *In search of mind: Essays in autobiography.* New York: Harper & Row.

Bushe, G. R., & Kassam, A. F. (2005). When is appreciative inquiry transformational? A meta-case analysis. *Journal of Applied Behavioral Science, 41*(2), 161–181. Accessed at www.gervasebushe.ca/ai-meta.pdf on June 15, 2011.

Buysse, V., Sparkman, K. L., & Wesley, P. W. (2003). Communities of practice: Connecting what we know with what we do. *Exceptional Children, 69*(3), 263–277.

Carroll, K. (2008, October 5). Connectivism squares with our experience [Web log post]. Accessed at http://ken-carroll.com/2008/10/05/connectivism-squares-with-our -experience/ on June 23, 2011.

Cassidy, K. (2008, July 5). Learning networks: My thinking thoughts [Web log post]. Accessed at http://primarypreoccupation.wordpress.com/2008/07/05/learning -networks-my-thinking-thoughts/ on June 23, 2011.

Catholic Relief Services. (2011). *Capacity building.* Accessed at http://crs.org/capacity -building/ on June 15, 2011.

Chen, Y., & Hoyle, J. R. (2007). *Teacher leadership in selected elementary schools in Texas: A distributed leadership perspective.* Accessed at www.ucea.org/storage /convention/convention2007/proceedings/Chen_UCEA2007.pdf on June 15, 2011.

Chinquapin Learning Edge. (n.d.). 2010 project outline [Wiki entry]. Accessed at http:// chinquapinlearningedge.wikispaces.com/2010+Project+Outline on August 23, 2011.

Cisco. (2007). The human network [Video file]. Accessed at www.youtube.com /watch?v=LFX8f_LqlZs&feature=player_embedded on June 15, 2011.

Coburn, C. E. (2003). Rethinking scale: Moving beyond numbers to deep and lasting change. *Educational Researcher, 32*(6), 3–12.

Cochran-Smith, M., & Lytle, S. L. (Eds). (1993). *Inside/outside: Teacher research and knowledge.* New York: Teachers College Press.

Cochran-Smith, M., & Lytle, S. L. (1999). Relationships of knowledge and practice: Teacher learning in communities. *Review of Research in Education, 24*(1), 249–305.

Collier, L. (2007). The shift to 21st-century literacies. *Council Chronicle, 17*(2), 4–8. Accessed at www.stenhouse.com/assets/pdfs/ccnov07shift.pdf on June 15, 2011.

Collins, A., Brown, J. S., & Newman, S. E. (1989). Cognitive apprenticeship: Teaching the craft of reading, writing, and mathematics. In L. B. Resnick (Ed.), *Knowing, learning, and instruction: Essays in honor of Robert Glaser* (pp. 453–494). Hillsdale, NJ: Erlbaum.

Conner, M. (2000). Linking, lurking, listening and learning: An interview with John Seely Brown. *LiNEZine.* Accessed at www.linezine.com/7.1/interviews/jsbmcl4.htm on August 23, 2011.

Conole, G., de Laat, M., Dillon, T., & Darby, J. (2006). *Student experiences of technologies.* Accessed at www.jisc.ac.uk/media/documents/programmes/elearningpedagogy /lxpprojectfinalreportdec06.pdf on January 10, 2008.

Cooperrider, D. L. (1996). Resources for getting appreciative inquiry started: An example OD proposal. *OD Practitioner, 28,* 23–33.

Cooperrider, D. L., & Whitney, D. (2005). Appreciative inquiry: A positive revolution in change. San Francisco: Berrett-Koehler.

Copland, M. A. (2003). Leadership of inquiry: Building and sustaining capacity for school improvement. *Educational Evaluation and Policy Analysis, 25*(4), 375–395.

Corbett, D., & Wilson, B. (1995). Make a difference with, not for, students: A plea to researchers and reformers. *Educational Researcher, 24*(5), 12–17.

Costa, C. (2007). The curriculum in a community of practice. *Educational Sciences Journal, 3,* 85–96. Accessed at http://sisifo.fpce.ul.pt/?r=12&p=85 on June 16, 2011.

Cothrel, J., & Williams, R. L. (1999). On-line communities: Helping them form and grow. *Journal of Knowledge Management, 3*(1), 54–60.

Couros, G. (n.d.). About. *The principal of change.* Accessed at http://georgecouros.ca/blog /about-me on June 24, 2011.

Couros, G. (2010, April 12). Changing leadership together [Web log post]. Accessed at http://georgecouros.ca/blog/archives/167 on June 24, 2011.

Cripe, D., Kelly, B., Moore, M., Place, C., & Preston, C. (2011). Forest hills nagel team 1. *Powerful learning practice.* Accessed at http://plpohiodallas10.wikispaces.com /Forest+Hills+Nagel+Team+1 on June 24, 2011.

Cripe's Chronicles. (2010, May 16). Bring your own device initiative: How it changed my classroom [Web log post]. Accessed at http://blogs.foresthills.edu /mrscripe/2011/05/16/bring-your-own-device-initiative-how-it-changed-my -classroom/ on June 24, 2011.

Dalgarno, N., & Colgan, L. (2007). Supporting novice elementary mathematics teachers' induction in professional communities and providing innovative forms of pedagogical content knowledge development through information and communication technology. *Teaching and Teacher Education, 23*(7), 1051–1065.

Dana, N. F., & Yendol-Hoppey, D. (2008). *The reflective educator's guide to professional development: Coaching inquiry-oriented learning communities.* Thousand Oaks, CA: Corwin Press.

Darken, R. P., & Sibert, J. L. (1996, April). *Way finding strategies and behaviors in large virtual worlds.* Paper presented at the Conference on Human Factors in Computing Systems, Vancouver, British Columbia. Accessed at http://sigchi.org/chi96 /proceedings/papers/Darken/Rpd_txt.htm on January 10, 2008.

Darling-Hammond, L., & Richardson, N. (2009). Teacher learning: What matters? *Educational Leadership, 66*(5), 46–53.

Darling-Hammond, L., Wei, R. C., Andree, A., Richardson, N., & Orphanos, S. (2009). *Professional learning in the learning profession: A status report on teacher development in the United States and abroad.* Accessed at www.srnleads.org /resources/publications/nsdc/nsdc_2009-02_execsumm.pdf on June 23, 2011.

Davenport, E., & Hall, H. (2002). Organizational knowledge and communities of practice. *Annual Review of Information Science and Technology, 36*(1), 171–227.

Dede, C. (2003). No cliché left behind: Why education policy is not like the movies. *Educational Technology, 43*(2), 5–10. Accessed at www.ncrel.org/tech/netc/2002 /present.htm on September 2, 2010.

Dede, C., Breit, L., Ketelhut, D. J., McCloskey, E., &Whitehouse, P. (2005). *An overview of current findings from empirical research on online teacher professional development.* Accessed at http://citeseerx.ist.psu.edu/viewdoc/download?doi=10.1.1.117 .1285&rep=rep1&type=pdfon June 16, 2011.

Dede, C., & Rockman, S. (2007, Spring). Lessons learned from studying how innovations can achieve scale. *Threshold*, 4–10.

de Kunder, M. (n.d.). The size of the World Wide Web. Accessed at www.worldwideweb size.com on September 10, 2010.

Dewey, J. (1897). My pedagogic creed. *School Journal, 54,* 77–80. Accessed at http://dewey .pragmatism.org/creed.htm on August 16, 2011.

Diigo. (2011). Wikipedia. Accessed at http://en.wikipedia.org/wiki/Diigo on January 10, 2011.

Donaldson, G. A. (2007). What do teachers bring to leadership? *Educational Leadership.* 65(1), 26–29. Accessed at www.ascd.org/publications/educational-leadership /sept07/vol65/num01/What-Do-Teachers-Bring-to-Leadership%C2%A2.aspx on June 16, 2011.

Downes, S. (2006). *Learning networks and connective knowledge.* Accessed at http://it.coe .uga.edu/itforum/paper92/paper92.html on January 10, 2008.

Downes, S. (2007a). Virtual and physical [Web log post]. Accessed at http://halfanhour .blogspot.com/2007/06/virtual-and-physical.html on June 21, 2011.

Downes, S. (2007b). What connectivism is [Web log post]. Accessed at http://halfanhour
    .blogspot.com/2007/02/what-connectivism-is.html on June 16, 2011.

Downes, S. (2009, December 4). Re: The reciprocity economy [Web log post comment].
    Accessed at http://nogoodreason.typepad.co.uk/no_good_reason/2009/04
    /the-reciprocity-economy.html?cid=6a00d8341c0c0e53ef01156f1ec449970c#co
    mment-6a00d8341c0c0e53ef01156f1ec449970c on June 16, 2011.

Downes, T., Fluck, A., Gibbons, P., Leonard, R., Matthews, C., Oliver, R., et al. (2002).
    *Making better connections: Models of teacher professional development for the
    integration of information and communication technology into classroom practice.*
    Canberra, Australia: Department of Education, Science and Training.

DuFour, R. (2004). What is a "professional learning community"? *Educational Leadership,
    61*(8), 6–11.

DuFour, R. (2007, November). In praise of top-down leadership. *School Administrator.*
    Accessed at www.aasa.org/publications/saarticledetail.cfm?ItemNumber=9540
    &snItemNumber=950&tnItemNumber= on June 10, 2010

DuFour, R. (2009). The key to improved teaching and learning. *AdvancED Source.*
    Accessed at www.allthingsplc.info/pdf/articles/the_key_to_improved
    _teaching_and_learning.pdf on June 17, 2011.

DuFour, R., DuFour, R., Eaker, R., & Many, T. (2006a). *Learning by doing: A handbook
    for professional learning communities at work.* Bloomington, IN: Solution Tree
    Press.

DuFour, R., DuFour, R., Eaker, R., & Many, T. (2006b). *Making time for collaboration.*
    Accessed at www.allthingsplc.info/pdf/articles/MakingTimeforCollaboration.pdf
    on June 17, 2011.

Dunbar's Number. (2011). Wikipedia. Accessed at http://en.wikipedia.org/wiki/Dunbar
    %27s_number on June 23, 2011.

Elmore, R. F., Peterson, P. L., & McCarthey, S. J. (1996). *Restructuring in the classroom:
    Teaching learning, and school organization.* San Francisco: Jossey-Bass.

Empowered educators. (n.d.). *National High School Alliance.* Accessed at www.hsalliance
    .org/call_action/empowered_educators/research.asp on April 13, 2011.

Fahey, K. (n.d.). *Collaborative inquiry: The view from the district office.* Accessed at www
    .nsrfharmony.org/research_fahey.pdf on June 17, 2011.

Ferrance, E. (2000). *Action research.* Providence, RI: Northeast and Islands Regional
    Educational Laboratory.

Ferriter, W. (2010, November 9). The power of PLCs [Web log post]. Accessed at http://
    teacherleaders.typepad.com/the_tempered_radical/2010/11/the-power-of-plcs
    .html on June 17, 2011.

Fisch, K. (2008, November 26). Take a learning posture [Web log post]. Accessed at http://
    plpnetwork.com/2008/11/26/take-a-learning-posture/ on June 23, 2011.

Fisch, K. (2010, April 8). One toe back in the classroom [Web log post]. Accessed at http://thefischbowl.blogspot.com/2010/04/one-toe-back-in-classroom.html on June 23, 2011.

Fisch, K. (2011, June 17). Transparent algebra: Take two [Web log post]. Accessed at http://thefischbowl.blogspot.com/search/label/transparent_algebra on June 23, 2011.

Fisher, C. (2007, August 29). School begins . . . But not here [Web log post]. Accessed at www.evenfromhere.org/?p=328 on June 23, 2011.

Fisher, C. (2008, September 12). Live in the classroom! [Web log post]. Accessed at www.evenfromhere.org/?p=140 on June 23, 2011.

Fletcher, A. (2005). *Meaningful student involvement: Guide to students as partners in school change* (2nd ed.). Bothell, WA: HumanLinks Foundation. Accessed at www.soundout.org/MSIGuide.pdf on June 17, 2011.

Fontaine, M. (2001). Keeping communities of practice afloat. *Knowledge Management Review, 4*(4), 16–21.

Freire, P. (1970). *Pedagogy of the oppressed.* New York: Continuum International.

Frost, D., & Durrant, J. (2003). Teacher leadership: Rationale, strategy and impact. *School Leadership and Management, 23*(2), 173–186.

Fullan, M. (1993). *Change forces: Probing the depths of educational reform.* London: Falmer Press.

Fullan, M. (1994). Teacher leadership: A failure to conceptualize leadership. In D. R. Walling. (Ed.), *Teachers as leaders: Perspectives on the professional development of teachers* (pp. 241–253). Bloomington, IN: Phi Delta Kappa Educational Foundation.

Fullan, M. (2001a). *Leading in a culture of change.* San Francisco: Jossey Bass.

Fullan, M. (2001b). *The new meaning of educational change* (3rd ed.). New York: Teachers College Press.

Fullan, M. (2002). The change leader. *Educational Leadership, 59*(8), 16–21.

Fullan, M. (2006). Leading professional learning: Think 'system' and not 'individual school' if the goal is to fundamentally change the culture. *School Administrator.* Accessed at http://aasa.rd.net/publications/saarticledetail.cfm?mnitemnumber=&tnitemnumber=&itemnumber=7565&unitemnumber=&pf=1&snitemnumber= on March 15, 2011.

Fullan, M., & Hargreaves, A. (1991). *What's worth fighting for in your school?* Andover, MA: Regional Laboratory for Educational Improvement of the Northeast and Islands.

Gallucci, C. (2007). *Using sociocultural theory to link individual and organizational learning processes: The case of highline school district's instructional improvement reform.* Accessed at http://depts.washington.edu/ctpmail/PDFs/OrgLearningCG-01-2007.pdf on June 22, 2011.

Gehrke, N. (1991). *Developing teachers' leadership skills.* Washington DC: Office of Educational Research and Improvement. (ERIC Document Reproduction Service No. ED330691)

Gherardi, S., & Nicolini, D. (2002). Learning in a constellation of interconnected practices: Canon or dissonance? *Journal of Management Studies, 39*(4), 419–436.

Goddard, Y. L., Goddard, R. D., & Tschannen-Moran, M. (2007). A theoretical and empirical investigation of teacher collaboration for school improvement and student achievement in public elementary schools. *Teachers College Record, 109*(4), 877–896.

Godin, S. (2010). *Linchpin: Are you indispensable?* New York: Portfolio Hardcover.

Grayson, P. (2011). Powerful learning—Put into practice [Web log post]. Accessed at http://plpnetwork.com/2011/05/06/powerful-learning-%E2%80%93-put-into-practice/ on June 23, 2011.

Grimmett, P. P., Erickson, G. L., Mackinnon, A. A., & Riecken, T. J. (1990). Reflective practice in teacher education. In R. T. Clift, W. R. Houston, & M. C. Pugach (Eds.), *Encouraging reflective practice in education: An analysis of issues and programs* (pp. 20–38). New York: Teachers College Press.

Grosseck, G., & Holotescu, C. (2009). Indicators for the analysis of learning and practice communities from the perspective of microblogging as a provocative sociolect in virtual space. *The 5th international scientific conference: elearning and software for education.* Accessed at http://adlunap.ro/else2009/journal/Lucrari/23-1050.1.GrosseckHolotescu.pdf on April 18, 2010.

Guldberg, K., & Pilkington, R. (2006). A community of practice approach to the development of non-traditional learners through networked learning. *Journal of Computer Assisted Learning, 22*(3), 159–171.

Gunawardena, C. N., Lowe, C. A., & Anderson, T. (1997). Analysis of a global online debate and the development of an interaction analysis model for examining social construction of knowledge in computer conferencing. *Journal of Educational Computing Research, 17*(4), 397–431.

Hagel, J., Brown, J. S., & Davison, L. (2010). *The power of pull: How small moves, smartly made, can set big things in motion.* New York: Basic Books.

Hall, G. E., & Hord, S. M. (1987). *Change in schools: Facilitating the process.* Albany: State University of New York Press.

Hall, G., & Hord, S. (2006). *Implementing change: Patterns, principles, and potholes.* Boston: Pearson/Allyn & Bacon.

Hall, G. & Loucks, S. (1979). *Implementing innovations in schools: A concerns-based approach* [Research and development report]. Austin: Research and Development Center for Teacher Education, University of Texas.

Hammond, S. (n.d). *What is appreciative inquiry?* Accessed at www.thinbook.com/docs/doc-whatisai.pdf on January 15, 2011.

Hargreaves, A. (1994). *Changing teachers, changing times: Teachers' work and culture in the postmodern age.* London: Cassell.

Hargreaves, A. (2004, January). *Educational change over time? The sustainability and nonsustainability of decades of secondary school change and continuity.* Keynote address presented at the Seventeenth Conference of the International Congress for School Effectiveness and Improvement, Rotterdam, Netherlands.

Hargreaves, D. (2004, July). *Transforming teaching and learning through ICT.* Paper presented at the Education.au Conference, Sydney, Australia.

Harris, A. (2002). *School improvement: What's in it for schools?* London: RoutledgeFalmer.

Harris, A. (2003). Teacher leadership as distributed leadership: Heresy, fantasy or possibility? *School Leadership and Management, 23*(3), 313–324.

Harris, A. (2004). Distributed leadership and school improvement: Leading or misleading? *Educational Management Administration & Leadership, 32*(1), 11–24.

Harris, A. (2011). *The case for distributed leadership.* Accessed at www.ssat-inet.net/en-gb/resources/Pages/olc/papers/thecasefordistributed.aspx on June 22, 2011.

Harris, C. (2007). Five reasons not to blog. *School Library Journal, 53*(4). Accessed at www.schoollibraryjournal.com/article/CA6430167.html on June 22, 2011.

Henri, F., & Pudelko, B. (2003). Understanding and analysing activity and learning in virtual communities. *Journal of Computer Assisted Learning, 19*(4), 474–487.

Hollins, E. R., McIntyre, L. R., DeBose, C. Hollins, K. S., & Towner, A. (2004). Promoting a self-sustaining learning community: Investigating an internal model for teacher development. *International Journal of Qualitative Studies in Education, 17*(2), 247–264.

Hord, S. (1997). *Professional learning communities: Communities of continuous inquiry and improvement.* Austin, TX: Southwest Educational Development Laboratory. Accessed at www.sedl.org/pubs/change34/plc-cha34.pdf on June 22, 2011.

Hord, S., & Sommers, W. A. (2008). *Leading professional learning communities: Voices from research and practice.* Thousand Oaks: Corwin Press.

Hunter, D., Bailey, A., & Taylor, B. (1995). *The art of facilitation.* Auckland, New Zealand: Tandem Press.

IEL. (2001). *Leadership for student learning: Redefining the teacher as leader.* Accessed at www.iel.org/programs/21st/reports/teachlearn.pdf on June 22, 2011.

Illich, I. (1970). *Deschooling society.* London: Calder & Boyars.

International Society for Technology in Education. (2008). *Standards: NETS for teachers.* Accessed at www.iste.org/Content/NavigationMenu/NETS/ForTeachers/2008Standards/NETS_T_Standards_Final.pdf on June 22, 2011.

International Society for Technology in Education. (2009). *Standards: NETS for administrators.* Accessed at www.iste.org/Content/NavigationMenu/NETS/ForAdministrators/2009Standards/NETS-A_2009.pdf on January 27, 2011.

Ivanova, M. (2009, April). *From personal learning environment building to professional learning network forming.* Paper presented at the 5th International Scientific Conference: eLearning and Software for Education, Bucharest, Romania. Accessed at http://adlunap.ro/else2009/papers/1001.1.Ivanova.pdf on June 22, 2011.

Iverson, J. O., & McPhee, R. D. (2002). Knowledge management in communities of practice: Being true to the communicative character of knowledge. *Management Communication Quarterly, 16*(2), 259–266.

Jenkins, H. (2006). *Confronting the challenges of participatory culture: Media education for the 21st century.* Accessed at www.newmedialiteracies.org/files/working/NMLWhitePaper.pdf on June 22, 2011.

Jeppesen, L. B., & Frederiksen, L., (2006). Why do users contribute to firm-hosted user communities? The case of computer-controlled music instruments. *Organization Science, 17*(1), 45–63.

John Holt. (2011). Wikipedia. Accessed at http://en.wikipedia.org/wiki/John_Holt_%28educator%29 on August 2, 2011.

Johnson, C. M. (2001). A survey of current research on online communities of practice. *Internet and Higher Education, 4*(1), 45–60.

Johnson, L., Levine, A., & Smith, R. (2009). *The 2009 horizon report.* Austin, Texas: New Media Consortium.

Johnson, S. (2008). *The invention of air: A story of science, faith, revolution, and the birth of America.* New York: Riverhead Books.

Katzenmeyer, M., & Moller, G. (2009). *Awakening the sleeping giant: Helping teachers develop as leaders* (3rd ed.). Thousand Oaks, CA: Corwin Press.

Kaufman, W. (2010). At Amazon, e-book sales outpace hardbacks. *NPR.* Accessed at www.npr.org/templates/story/story.php?storyId=128635547 on June 22, 2011.

Kearsley, G. (2011a). *Social development theory.* Accessed at http://tip.psychology.org/vygotsky.html on June 23, 2011.

Keasley, G. (2011b). *Theory into practice.* Accessed at http://tip.psychology.org/lave.html on June 23, 2011.

Kilgore, S. B., & Reynolds, K. J. (2011). *From silos to systems: Reframing schools for success.* Thousand Oaks, CA: Corwin Press.

King, B. (2009). Drinking from the fire hose: Finding useful drops in the Twitter deluge. *Seybold Report: Analyzing Publishing Technologies, 9*(6), 14. Accessed at http://connection.ebscohost.com/c/articles/37286347/drinking-from-fire-hose-finding-useful-drops-twitter-deluge on June 22, 2011.

Kling, R., & Courtright, C. (2003). Group behaviour and learning in electronic forums: A sociocultural approach. *Information Society, 19*(3), 221–235.

Knapp, M. S., McCaffrey, T., & Swanson, J. (2003, April). *District support for professional learning; What research says and has yet to establish.* Paper presented at the Annual Meeting of the American Educational Research Association, Chicago, Illinois.

Kruse, S. D., Louis, K. S., & Bryk, A. S. (1995). An emerging framework for analyzing school-based professional community. In K. S. Louis & S. Kruse (Eds.), *Professionalism and community: Perspectives on reforming urban schools* (pp. 23–42). Thousand Oaks, CA: Corwin Press.

Lai, K. W., Pratt, K., Anderson, M., & Stigter, J. (2006). *Literature review and synthesis: Online communities of practice.* Accessed at www.educationcounts.govt.nz /publications/curriculum/5795 on June 22, 2011.

Lambert, L. (1998). *Building leadership capacity in schools.* Alexandria, VA: Association for Supervision and Curriculum Development.

Lave, J. (1991). Situated learning in communities of practice. In L. Resnick, J. M. Levine, & S. D. Teasley (Eds.), *Perspectives on socially shared cognition* (pp. 63–82). Washington, DC: American Psychological Association.

Lave, J., & Wenger, E. (1991). *Situated learning: Legitimate peripheral participation.* New York: Cambridge University Press.

Lee, D. (2006). Roles in CoP's [Web log post]. *The learning circuit blog.* Accessed at http:// learningcircuits.blogspot.com/2006/06/roles-in-cops.html on June 22, 2011.

Leithwood, K., Louis, K. S., Anderson, S., & Wahlstrom, K. (2004). *How leadership influences student learning.* Accessed at www.wallacefoundation.org/SiteCollection Documents/WF/Knowledge%20Center/Attachments/PDF/HowLeadership Influences.pdf on June 22, 2011.

Leithwood, K., Steinbach, R., & Jantzi, D. (2002). School leadership and teachers' motivation to implement accountability policies. *Educational Administration Quarterly, 38*(1), 94–119.

Lenhardt, A., & Madden, M. (2005). Teen content creators and consumers. *Pew Internet & American Life Project.* Accessed at www.pewInternet.org/PPF/r/166/report _display.asp on June 22, 2011.

Lewis, J. H., & Romiszowski, A. (1996). Networking and the learning organization: Networking issues and scenarios for the 21st century. *Journal of Instructional Science and Technology, 1*(4). Accessed at www.usq.edu.au/electpub/e-jist/docs /old/vol1no4/contents.htm on March 31, 2009.

Lieberman, A. (2000). Networks as learning communities: Shaping the future of teacher development. *Journal of Teacher Education, 51*(3), 221–227.

Little, J. W. (1993). Teachers' professional development in a climate of educational reform. *Educational Evaluation and Policy Analysis, 15*(2), 129–151.

Little, J. W. (2000). Assessing the Prospects for Teacher Leadership. In *The Jossey-Bass Reader on Educational Leadership* (pp. 390–419). San Francisco: Jossey-Bass.

Lucier, R. (2010). When no 'one' you know knows, a connected educator knows that nodes know [Twitter post]. Accessed at http://twitter.com/thecleversheep on July 31, 2010.

MacIsaac, D. (2000). Communities of on-line physics educators. *Physics Teacher, 38*(4), 210–213.

Madden, M., Fox, S., Smith, A., & Vitak, J. (2007). Digital footprints. Accessed at http://pewinternet.org/Reports/2007/Digital-Footprints.aspx on August 10, 2011.

Manz, C. C. (1998). *The leadership wisdom of Jesus: Practical lessons for today.* San Francisco: Berrett-Koehler.

Martin-Kniep, G. O. (2008). Purposes and dispositions of professional learning communities. *Communities that learn, lead, and last: Building and sustaining educational expertise* (pp. 19–33). San Francisco: Jossey-Bass.

Maslow's Hierarchy of Needs. (2011). Wikipedia. Accessed at http://en.wikipedia.org/wiki/Maslow%27s_hierarchy_of_needs on June 23, 2011.

McDermott, R. (2001). *Knowing in community: 10 critical success factors in building communities of practice.* Accessed at www.co-i-l.com/coil/knowledge-garden/cop/knowing.shtml on June 22, 2011.

McElvaney, J., & Berge, Z. (2009). Weaving a personal web: Using online technologies to create customized, connected, and dynamic learning environments. *Canadian Journal of Learning and Technology, 35*(2). Accessed at www.cjlt.ca/index.php/cjlt/article/view/524/257 on June 14, 2011.

McLaughlin, M. W., & Talbert, J. E. (2001). *Professional communities and the work of high school teaching.* Chicago: University of Chicago Press.

McLaughlin, T. H. (2003). Teaching as a practice and a community of practice: The limits of commonality and the demands of diversity. *Journal of Philosophy of Education, 37*(2), 339–352.

Metiri Group. (n.d.). *enGauge 21st century skills for 21st century learners.* Accessed at www.metiri.com/21/Metiri-NCREL21stSkills.pdf on June 17, 2011.

Michaelsen, A. (2011, June 22). Global connections: My PLN story [Web blog post]. Accessed at http://plpnetwork.com/2011/06/22/global-connections-my-pln-story on August 23, 2011.

Mizell, H. (2007). District leadership: Students learn when adults learn. *The Learning System, 3*(3). Accessed at www.nsdc.org/news/system/sys11-07mizell.pdf on June 22, 2011.

Muijs, D., & Harris, A. (2003). Teacher leadership—Improvement through empowerment? An overview of research. *Educational Management Administration &Leadership, 31*(4), 437–448.

National Council of Teachers of English. (n.d.). *The NCTE definition of 21st century literacies.* Accessed at www.ncte.org/positions/statements/21stcentdefinition on June 22, 2011.

National Council of Teachers of English. (2007). *21st-century literacies.* Accessed at www.ncte.org/library/NCTEFiles/Resources/Positions/Chron1107ResearchBrief.pdf on June 22, 2011.

National School Reform Faculty. (2008). What are the characteristics of a professional learning community? *Frequently asked questions.* Accessed at www.nsrfharmony.org/faq.html#1 on June 22, 2011.

Newhouse, C. P. (2001). Applying the concerns-based adoption model to research on computers in classrooms. *Journal of Research on Technology in Education, 33*(5). Accessed at www.iste.org/content/navigationmenu/publications/jrte/issues /volume_331/number_5_summer_2001/applying_the_concerns-based_adoption _model_to_research_on_computers_in_classrooms_part_i.htm on February 1, 2011.

Newton's Laws of Motion. (2011). Wikipedia. Accessed at http://en.wikipedia.org/wiki /Newton%27s_laws_of_motion on June 23, 2011.

Nichani, M., & Hung, D. (2002). Can a community of practice exist online? *Educational Technology, 42*(4), 49–54.

The Nielsen Company. (2010). *Blog Pulse.* Accessed at www.blogpulse.com on September 12, 2010.

Palincsar, A. S., Magnusson, S. J., Marano, N., Ford, D., & Brown, N. (1998). Designing a community of practice: Principles and practices of the GIsML community. *Teaching and Teacher Education, 14*(1), 5–19.

Palloff, R. M., & Pratt, K. (1999). *Building learning communities in cyberspace: Effective strategies for the online classroom.* San Francisco: Jossey-Bass.

Partnership for 21st Century Skills. (2009). *Framework for 21st century learning.* Accessed at www.p21.org/documents/P21_Framework.pdf on June 17, 2011.

Peterson, K. (1994). *Building collaborative cultures: Seeking ways to reshape urban schools* [NCREL Monograph]. Accessed at www.ncrel.org/sdrs/areas/issues/educatrs /leadrshp/le0pet.htm on June 22, 2011.

Peterson, K. (2002). *Enhancing school culture: Reculturing schools.* Accessed at http://smhp .psych.ucla.edu/qf/burnout_qt/reculturingschools.pdf on June 22, 2011.

Piaget, J. (1962). *Play, dreams and imitation in childhood.* New York: Norton.

Piaget, J., & Inhelder, B. (1969). *The psychology of the child.* New York: Basic Books.

Pink, D. (2009). *Drive: The surprising truth about what motivates us.* New York: Penguin.

Postman, N. (1992). *Technopoly: The surrender of culture to technology.* New York: Knopf.

Preece, J. (2000). *Online communities: Designing usability, supporting sociability.* New York: Wiley.

Preece, J. (2004). Etiquette, empathy and trust in communities of practice: Stepping-stones to social capital. *Journal of Universal Computer Science, 10*(3), 294–302. Accessed at www.jucs.org/jucs_10_3/etiquette_empathy_and_trust/Preece_J.pdf on June 22, 2011.

Prensky, M. (2001). *Digital game-based learning.* New York: McGraw Hill.

Project Tomorrow. (2010). *Creating our future: Students speak up about their visions for 21st century learning.* Accessed at www.tomorrow.org/speakup/pdfs/SU09Natio nalFindingsStudents&Parents.pdf on June 22, 2011.

Ramaswamy, R., Storer, G., & Van Zeyl, R. (2005). Designing sustainable communities of practice at CARE. *KM4D Journal, 1*(1),79–93. Accessed at http://journal.km4dev .org/index.php/km4dj/article/view/16/11 on June 22, 2011.

Rasberry, M., & Mahajan, G. (2008). *From isolation to collaboration: Promoting teacher leadership through PLCs.* Hillsborough, NC: Center for Teaching Quality. (ERIC Document Reproduction Service No. ED503637)

Reason, P., & Riley, S. (2003). Co-operative inquiry: An action research practice. In J. A. Smith (Ed.), *Qualitative psychology: A practical guide to research methods* (pp. 207–234). Thousand Oaks, CA: SAGE. Accessed at http://people.bath.ac.uk /mnspwr/Papers/DoingCo-operativeInquiry.pdf on January 10, 2011.

Richardson, J. (2005). Transform your group into a team. *Tools for Schools, 9*(2), 1–8.

Riel, M., & Fulton, K. (2001). The role of technology in supporting learning communities. *Phi Delta Kappan, 82*(7), 518–523.

Riel, M., & Polin, L. (2004). Learning communities: Common ground and critical differences in designing technical support. In S. A. Barab, R. Kling, & J. H. Gray (Eds.), *Designing for virtual communities in the service of learning* (pp. 2–50). New York: Cambridge University Press.

Ritter-Hall, L. (2010, January 26). Taking one step, then another, to an entirely new level [Web log post]. Accessed at http://plpnetwork.com/2010/01/26/taking-one-step -then-another-to-an-entirely-new-level/ on June 23, 2011.

Robertson, J., & Strachan, J. (2001). Teachers taking leadership. In C. McGee & D. Fraser (Eds.), *The professional practice of teaching* (2nd ed., pp. 320–334). Palmerston North, NZ: Dunmore Press.

Schank, R., (2004). Schanks law. *Edge.* Accessed at http://edge.org/response-detail/2112 /whats-your-law on June 23, 2011.

Schecter, S., Golanka, S., Johnson, K., Soloff, E., Rosenblatt, N., Moonga, H., et al. (2011). Trevor Day School. *Powerful learning practice.* Accessed at http://plpadvis .wikispaces.com/Trevor+Day+School on June 24, 2011.

Schlager, M. S., & Fusco, J. (2004). Teacher professional development, technology, and communities of practice: Are we putting the cart before the horse? In S. Barab, R. Kling, & J. Gray (Eds.) *Designing for virtual communities in the service of learning* (pp. 120–153). New York: Cambridge University Press.

Schmoker, M. (2004). Tipping point: From feckless reform to substantive instructional improvement. *Phi Delta Kappan, 85*(6), 424–432. Accessed at www.pdkintl.org /kappan/k0402sch.htm on June 23, 2011.

Schmoker, M. (2005). Here and now: Improving teaching and learning. In R. DuFour, R. Eaker, & R. DuFour (Eds.), *On common ground* (pp. xi–xvi). Bloomington, IN: Solution Tree Press.

Schwen, T. M., & Hara, N. (2003). Community of practice: A metaphor for online design? *Information Society, 19*(3), 257–270.

Seel, R. (2008a). Appreciative inquiry. *New Paradigm Consulting.* Accessed at www .new-paradigm.co.uk/Appreciative.htm on June 23, 2011.

Seel, R. (2008b). Introduction to AI. *New Paradigm Consulting.* Accessed at www.new -paradigm.co.uk/introduction_to_ai.htm on June 23, 2011.

Senge, P. M. (1990a). *The fifth discipline: The art and practice of the learning organization.* New York: Doubleday/Currency.

Senge, P. M. (1990b). The leader's new work: Building learning organizations. *Sloan Management Review, 32*(1), 1–17.

Senge, P. M. (1997). Communities of leaders and learners. *Harvard Business Review, 75*(5), 30–31.

Senge, P. (2000). *Schools that learn: A fifth discipline fieldbook for educators, parents, and everyone who cares about education.* New York: Doubleday.

Sergiovanni, T. J. (1992). Why we should seek substitutes for leadership. *Educational Leadership, 49*(5), 41–45

Sergiovanni, T. J. (1999). Refocusing leadership to build community. *High School Magazine, 7*(1), 10–15.

Sharratt, M., & Usoro, A. (2003). Understanding knowledge-sharing in online communities of practice. *Electronic Journal of Knowledge Management, 1*(2), 18–27. Accessed at www.ejkm.com/volume-1/volume1-issue-2/issue2-art18-sharratt. pdf on April 13, 2005.

Shaughnessy, J., & Kushman, J. (1997). Research in the hands of students. In W. Kushman (Ed.), *Look who's talking now: Student views of learning in restructuring schools* (pp. 29–39). Portland, OR: Northwest Regional Educational Lab. Accessed at www.eric.ed.gov/PDFS/ED404752.pdf on June 23, 2011. (ERIC Document Reproduction Service No. ED404752)

Sherer, P. D., Shea, T. P., & Kristensen, E. (2003). Online communities of practice: A catalyst for faculty development. *Innovative Higher Education, 27*(3), 183–194.

Shirky, C. (2008). *Here comes everybody: The power of organizing without organizations.* New York: Penguin.

Shulman, L. S. (2004). *Teaching as community property: Essays on higher education.* San Francisco: Jossey-Bass.

Siemens, G. (2003). Learning ecology, communities, and networks: Extending the classroom. *elearnspace.* Accessed at www.elearnspace.org/Articles/learning_communities .htm on October 1, 2010.

Siemens, G. (2005a). Connectivism: Learning as network creation. *elearnspace.* Accessed at www.elearnspace.org/Articles/networks.htm on June 23, 2011.

Siemens, G. (2005b). *Connectivism: A learning theory for the digital age.* Accessed at www.itdl.org/Journal/Jan_05/article01.htm on June 23, 2011.

Siemens, G. (2006). *Knowing knowledge.* Accessed at http://ltc.umanitoba.ca /KnowingKnowledge/index.php/Main_Page on April 20, 2009.

Siemens, G. (2008). *Learning and knowing in networks: Changing roles for educators and designers.* Accessed at www.ipcp.org.br/References/Education/Siemens.pdf on June 23, 2011.

Siemens, G. (2009). Teaching as transparent learning [Web log post]. Accessed at www .connectivism.ca/?p=122 on June 23, 2011.

Siemens, G., & Downes, S. (2009). Connectivism. *Learning Technologies Centre.* Accessed at http://ltc.umanitoba.ca/wiki/Connectivism on July 27, 2010.

Smith, P. J. (2003). Workplace learning and flexible delivery. *Review of Educational Research, 73*(1), 53–88.

Sobero, P. M. (2008). Essential components for successful virtual learning communities. *Journal of Extension, 46*(4). Accessed at www.joe.org/joe/2008august/a1.php on June 23, 2011.

Starr, S. (n.d.). Creating and sustaining collaborative relationships among teachers. Accessed at www.educ.uvic.ca/epls/faculty/storey/Starr.htm on March 10, 2011.

Stoll, L., Bolam, R., McMahon, A., Wallace, M., & Thomas, S. (2006). Professional learning communities: A review of the literature. *Journal of Educational Change, 7*(4), 221–258.

Stuckey, B. (2001). *Literature review 2—Communities of practice.* Accessed at http://brink .uow.edu.au/~bstuckey/presentations/literature_2.PDF on March 9, 2005.

Stuckey, B., & Smith, J. D. (2004, March). *Sustaining communities of practice.* Paper presented at the International Association for Development of the Information Society Conference, Lisbon. Accessed at http://citeseerx.ist.psu.edu/viewdoc /download?doi=10.1.1.104.3258&rep=rep1&type=pdf on June 23, 2011.

Tapscott, D., & Williams, A. D. (2008). *Wikinomics: How mass collaboration changes everything.* New York: Portfolio.

Taylor, B. (2009, June 18). The 10 questions every change agent must answer [Web log post]. Accessed at http://blogs.hbr.org/taylor/2009/06/the_10_questions_every_change .html on June 24, 2011.

Toffler, A. (2011). *Toffler quotes.* Accessed at www.alvintoffler.net/?fa=galleryquotes on June 23, 2011.

Tschannen-Moran, M. (2011). Survey instruments to help you in your investigations of schools. Accessed at http://mxtsch.people.wm.edu/research_tools.php on August 11, 2011.

Tuckman, B. (1965). Developmental sequence in small groups. *Psychological Bulletin, 63,* 384–399.

U.S. Department of Education. (2011). The promise of communities of practice. Accessed at www.ed.gov/oii-news/promise-communities-practice on July 27, 2011.

Utecht, J. (2008). Stages of PLN adoption [Web log post]. Accessed at www.thethinkingstick .com/?p=652 on June 23, 2011.

Vescio, V., Ross, D., & Adams, A. (2008). A review of research on the impact of professional learning communities on teaching practice and student learning. *Teaching and Teacher Education, 24*(1), 80–91.

Warlick, D. (2007). *The art of cultivating a personal learning network* [Slide show]. Accessed at www.slideshare.net/dwarlick/personal-learning-networkson June 23, 2011.

Wasko, M. M., & Faraj, S. (2000). "It is what one does": Why people participate and help others in electronic communities of practice. *Journal of Strategic Information Systems, 9*(2), 155–173.

Wasley, P. A. (1991). *Teachers who lead: The rhetoric of reform and the realities of practice.* New York: Teachers College Press.

Waters, J., & Gasson, S. (2007, January). *Distributed knowledge construction in an online community of inquiry.* Paper presented at the 40th Hawaii International Conference on System Sciences, Big Island, Hawaii. Accessed at http://doi.ieeecomputersociety.org/10.1109/HICSS.2007.179 on June 23, 2011.

Weller, M. (2009). On economy as metaphor [Web log post]. Accessed at http://nogood reason.typepad.co.uk/no_good_reason/2009/04/on-economy-as-metaphor.html on June 23, 2011.

Wells, C., & Feun, L., (2007). Implementation of learning community principles: A study of six high schools. *NASSP Bulletin, 91*(2), 141–160.

Wenger, E. (1998). *Communities of practice: Learning, meaning, and identity.* New York: Cambridge University Press.

Wenger, E. (2000). Communities of practice and social learning systems. *Organization, 7*(2), 225–246.

Wenger, E. (2006). Communities of practice: A brief introduction. Accessed at www.ewenger.com/theory on August 3, 2011.

Wenger, E., McDermott, W., & Snyder, W. (2002). *Cultivating communities of practice: A guide to managing knowledge.* Boston: Harvard Business School Press.

Wenger, E. C., & Snyder, W. M. (2000). Communities of practice: The organizational frontier. *Harvard Business Review, 78*(1), 139–145.

Whitby, G. B. (2006). *Distributive leadership as an emerging concept.* Accessed at www.uow.edu.au/content/groups/public/@web/@educ/documents/doc/uow037839.pdf on June 23, 2011.

Wood, D. R. (2007). Professional learning communities: Teachers, knowledge, and knowing. *Theory Into Practice, 46*(4), 281–290.

Wright, A. (2007). *Glut: Mastering information through the ages.* Washington, DC: Joseph Henry Press.

Wright, S. (2011a, March 28). Five days [Web log post]. Accessed at http://shelleywright.wordpress.com/2011/03/28/five-days on June 23, 2011.

Wright, S. (2011b, March 19). An hour in the classroom of a tech teacher [Web log post]. Accessed at http://shelleywright.wordpress.com/2011/03/19/an-hour-in-the -classroom-of-a-tech-teacher on June 23, 2011.

Wright, S. (2011c, March 8). Synthesis [Web log post]. Accessed at http://shelleywright .wordpress.com/2011/03/08/synthesis on June 23, 2011.

Zhao, Y. (2009). *Catching up or leading the way: American education in the age of glo- balization.* Alexandria, VA: Association for Supervision and Curriculum Development.

Zinn, L. F. (1997, March). *Supports and barriers to teacher leadership: Reports of teacher leaders.* Paper presented at the annual meeting of the American Educational Research Association, Chicago, Illinois. Accessed at http://lsc-net.terc.edu/do /paper/8120/show/use_set-careers/page-1.html on June 23, 2011.

Index

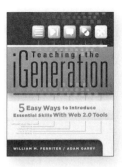

Teaching the iGeneration:
5 Easy Ways to Introduce Essential Skills With Web 2.0 Tools
William M. Ferriter and Adam Garry

Find the natural overlap between the work you already believe in and the digital tools that define tomorrow's learning. Each chapter introduces an enduring life skill and a digital solution to enhance traditional skill-based instructional practices. A collection of handouts and supporting materials ends each chapter.

BKF393

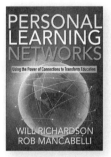

Personal Learning Networks:
Using the Power of Connections to Transform Education
Will Richardson and Rob Mancabelli

Follow this road map for using the web for learning. Learn how to build your own learning network. Use learning networks in the classroom and make the case for schoolwide learning networks to improve student outcomes.

BKF484

Creating a Digital-Rich Classroom:
Teaching & Learning in a Web 2.0 World
Meg Ormiston

Design and deliver standards-based lessons in which technology plays an integral role. This book provides a research base and practical strategies for using Web 2.0 tools to create engaging lessons that transform and enrich content.

BKF385

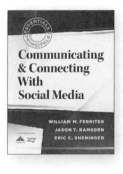

Communicating & Connecting With Social Media
William M. Ferriter, Jason T. Ramsden, and Eric C. Sheninger

In this short text, the authors examine how enterprising schools are using social media tools to provide customized professional development for teachers and to transform communication practices with staff, students, parents, and other stakeholders.

BKF474

Mobile Learning Devices
Kipp D. Rogers

Learn exactly what mobile learning is, how to introduce MLDs into your school, and ensure that teachers and students use them appropriately to enhance 21st century learning. Logistical implementation tips and examples of effective lesson plans are included.

BKF445

Solution Tree | Press

a division of
Solution Tree

Visit solution-tree.com or call 800.733.6786 to order.